D1518556

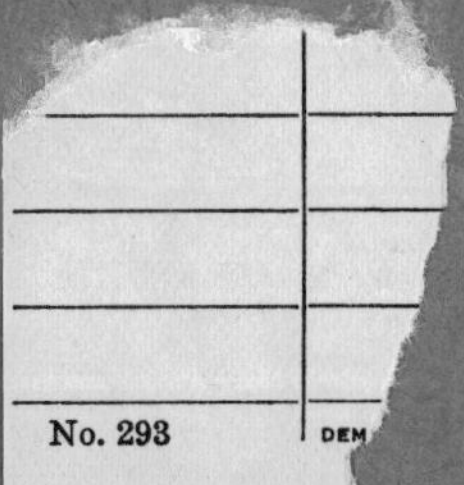
No. 293
DEM

HEADLINE BOOKS

No. 20

HEADLINE BOOKS

MADE IN U. S. A.

DICTATORSHIP

PEACE IN PARTY PLATFORMS

AMERICA CONTRADICTS HERSELF
The Story of Our Foreign Policy

COOPERATIVES

BILLIONS FOR DEFENSE

CHURCH AND STATE

CHANGING GOVERNMENTS
Amid New Social Problems

PEACEFUL CHANGE—
The Alternative to War

WAR IN CHINA
America's Role in the Far East

THE PUZZLE OF PALESTINE

SHADOW OVER EUROPE
The Challenge of Nazi Germany

BRICKS WITHOUT MORTAR
The Story of International Cooperation

THE GOOD NEIGHBORS
The Story of the Two Americas

BATTLES WITHOUT BULLETS
The Story of Economic Warfare

IN QUEST OF EMPIRE
The Problem of Colonies

HUMAN DYNAMITE
The Story of Europe's Minorities

HOUSING EUROPE
(In Preparation)

HUMAN DYNAMITE

THE STORY OF EUROPE'S MINORITIES

by

HENRY C. WOLFE

MAPS AND CHARTS BY
EMIL HERLIN

THE FOREIGN POLICY ASSOCIATION

Published October 1939

Typography by Andor Braun

COMPOSED, PRINTED AND BOUND BY UNION LABOR
MANUFACTURED IN THE UNITED STATES OF AMERICA

 1

CONTENTS

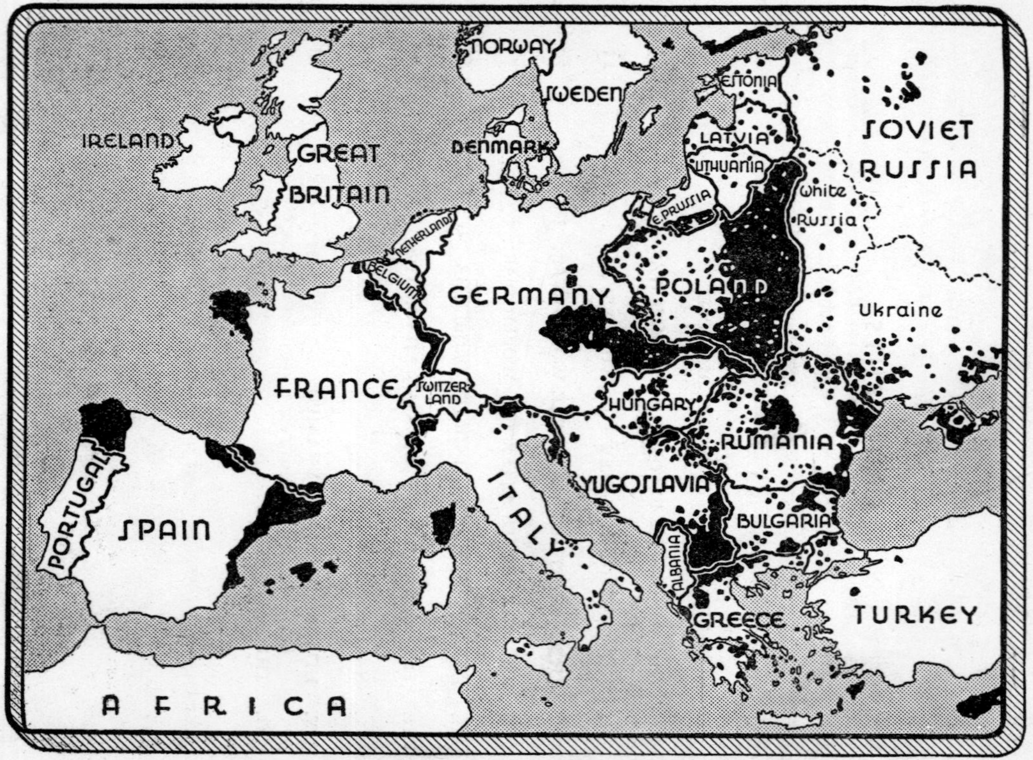

WHERE EUROPE'S PRINCIPAL MINORITY GROUPS ARE

I. What the Book Is About

The word "minority" has come to have a sinister sound. It has become associated with discord and disruption. During the past twenty years we have heard a great deal about Europe's minority problems. But few of us understand just what these problems are, or what they mean to us.

Stories of the refugees from Central Europe bring home to us the human side of the minority problem. But its underlying causes are political, economic, social—and enormously complicated. So, when we happened to notice a newspaper headline about a quarrel between the minority and majority peoples in some little-known part of Europe, most of us glanced at it indifferently and then turned to the sports page. It all seemed so unreal, so far away, so unimportant.

Yet these far-off minority troubles *are* important, and they have a way of coming home to us right here in these United States—sometimes with a bang.

MINORITY DISPUTES AND WAR

How? Well, take the World War, for example. That war grew in part out of a long minority quarrel between the Serbs on the one hand and the Austrians and Magyars (pronounced *mod*-yors) on the other. The quarrel reached a climax in the murder of the Austrian Archduke Franz Ferdinand at Sarajevo, down in the Balkans. That fatal shooting in a little Bosnian town set in motion a train of events which eventually brought even the United States into the fighting in Europe. Similarly it was in part, at least, a dispute about the German minority in Poland which started the new European war.

Of course, not all minority disputes end in war. But even when they do not, they have a profound effect on international relations. They have brought incalculable economic losses and have delayed the establishment of normal, civilized cultural and commercial relations between peoples and governments. They have stimulated the armaments race. They have caused an enormous amount of suffering to many of the minority peoples.

In some cases whole groups have been forced into flight from their homelands and have been obliged to seek refuge in countries that could ill afford to shelter them. In other cases minority disputes have led states to close their frontiers, causing financial losses and much bad feeling. Furthermore, some states have conducted propaganda campaigns which have kindled hatred and suspicion among peoples of differing ancestry. All this hatred and suspicion have helped to dry up international trade, made states the world over feel obliged to arm to the teeth, imposed heavy burdens on taxpayers and citizens high and low, and put pretty nearly all of us in a state of nervousness and foreboding.

So, whether minority strife takes place in the Balkans, along the Danube or in the Baltic area, and whether or not it results in war, it has a bearing on our welfare right here in America.

WHAT THIS BOOK TRIES TO DO

In this little book we shall try to approach the minorities problem objectively. We have no intention of championing the cause of any minority, or the claims of minorities against majorities in general. What we do hope to do is to give you a better understanding of this immensely important problem.

In taking up our subject, then, we shall first look at the map of Europe and see where the principal minorities are. Then we shall discover something about how these minorities came into existence. When we have done that, we can follow the history of Europe's minorities in the years before the World War and see how the peace treaties that were signed after the war affected the position of those minority peoples.

Once we have got an idea of this historical background, we shall set off on a tour of Europe, going from the states along the cold Baltic Sea to the warm lands of the Mediterranean and on to the Soviet Union, visiting the most important minorities and learning something about them and their points of view. When we have finished our tour we shall be in a better position to consider the efforts that have been made to solve the minority problems since the peace treaties were signed. Finally, we shall look into the most important of all Europe's minorities problems—the problem of Nazi Germany and her relations with the Germans living outside the borders of the German Reich. For it was Europe's failure to solve this problem in time which was one of the underlying causes of the present war.

So much for the preliminaries. Now for our story.

II. How the Minority Problem Arose

To show the extent to which Europe's minorities are scattered and the various branches of its population mixed, suppose you take an uncolored map of that continent. Now blindfold yourself, open a box of water colors, and start dabbing paint at random on the map. You will soon have the map spotted with green, yellow, blue, red, brown and other tints, from the Bay of Biscay in the west to the Ural Mountains in the east, and from the Arctic Ocean in the north to the Black and Mediterranean Seas in the south. You will have a child's idea of the map of Europe.

Now compare that specimen of slap-dab map-making with a good map of Europe on which the various nationalities are indicated by individual colors. The black, for instance, represents Germans. But is the black confined to the borders of the "Fatherland"? By no means. Dabs of black loom up unexpectedly in France, Switzerland and Belgium in the western part of Europe. There is a patch of black in northern Italy. Black spots of various sizes leave a trail right from the borders of Germany along the eastern shore of the Baltic and along the Gulf of Finland into the Soviet Union in the neighborhood of Leningrad. Patches of black bob up in all the countries which border the Danube. We find them sprinkled across Poland, the Russian Ukraine and in the Crimea (see the map on page 27). Even in Soviet Russia along the Volga and in the Caucasus mountains near the borders of Turkey and Iraq there are German minorities.

Of course the German minority situation is exceptional. No other people in Europe is so widely scattered. But we should remember that it is not always possible for a people to be gathered together in one state. On our imaginary map there are red, blue, green and other colors daubed here and there over most of the continent. The map that you blindly spattered with paint is not, after all, so absurd. The patches of color are almost certainly not correctly sized or placed but they give you an idea of the crazy-quilt of peoples and nationalities scattered throughout Europe. Though we have no color map in this book you can get some idea of how widespread Europe's minorities are from our frontispiece map (p. 6), as well as from the chart on page 11.

Another important point to keep in mind is that the map of Europe changes from time to time, and that as it changes minority groups become parts of majority groups, and parts of majority groups become minority groups. In other words, the minority situation is not fixed: it is always changing.

HOW EUROPE'S MINORITIES CAME TO BE

These little minority patches had their beginnings a long way back in history, when the peoples of Europe and Asia were

MINORITY PEOPLES IN EUROPE

(AS PERCENTAGES OF TOTAL POPULATIONS OF THEIR STATES)*

EACH SYMBOL REPRESENTS 10% OF TOTAL POPULATION OF STATE NAMED
BLACK REPRESENTS MAJORITY PEOPLES
WHITE REPRESENTS MINORITY PEOPLES

	MINORITIES
BELGIUM	.7%
DENMARK	1.7%
ITALY	1.9%
FRANCE	8.5%
GERMANY	9.4%
GREECE	11.3%
FINLAND	13.0%
BULGARIA	14.8%
ALBANIA	16.5%
HUNGARY	16.9%
YUGOSLAVIA	18.1%
ESTONIA, LATVIA, LITHUANIA	18.9%
SPAIN	21.4%
RUMANIA	26.1%
POLAND	30.7%
EUROPEAN TURKEY	40.8%
U.S.S.R. (EUROPE AND ASIA)	47.2%

*All figures are approximate, being based on the last census or the best available estimate.

frequently on the march. Look at the map on page 13 and you will get some idea of what a drastic reshuffling of these peoples took place in the first seven centuries after Christ.

THE MIGRATIONS CREATE MINORITIES

Nearly all the northern and eastern peoples who came down into Europe in those early days left their imprints where they passed and settled. Even the Asiatic tides which receded left their marks on the map of Europe. All over Russia today, for example, there are living reminders of the great Tartar invasions. That is the origin of the expression: "Scratch a Russian and you find a Tartar."

The Magyars, another people of Asiatic origin, came to the middle Danube a thousand years ago. Unlike the Tartars, they stayed in Europe, intermarried with the local peoples and founded a nation that is the Hungary of today.

Several centuries later the conquering Turks swept through the Slavic, Greek and Latin peoples of the Balkans, reaching the walls of Vienna in 1683. Though they were checked and eventually turned back, the Turks left the marks of their long rule in every Balkan region.

The Turkish colonies that were left in the Balkans when the Turks were driven back toward Constantinople are good examples of "minority islands." They are small, isolated groups of Turks living in the midst of the majority populations of Bulgaria, Yugoslavia, Rumania, Albania and Greece. These Turkish minority colonies have been duplicated many times in other parts of Europe by Ukrainians, Magyars, Lithuanians, Germans and other peoples whose minority islands have survived amid the ruling majority populations of the countries in which they live (see frontispiece map).

The religious and dynastic wars of the Middle Ages and the conflicts between states in modern times have created still other minorities. Almost every major war and many of the

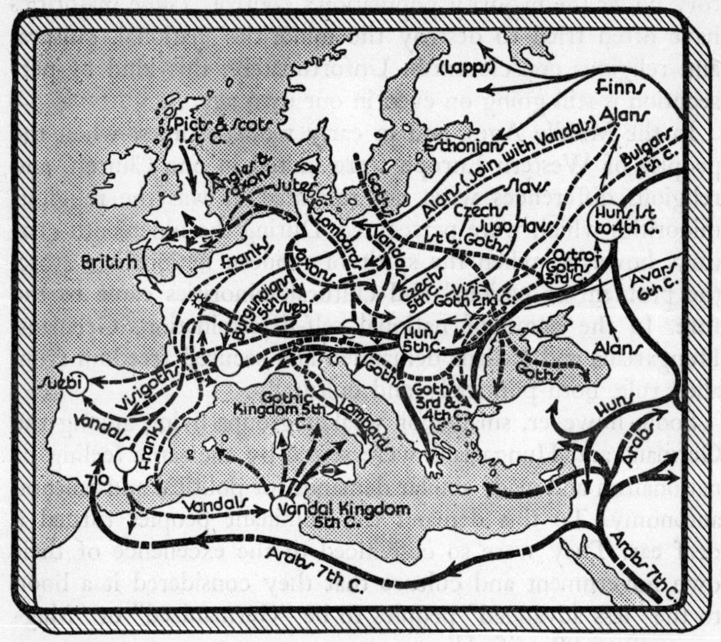

Based on a map in *The Outline of History*, by H. G. Wells. By permission.

THE GREAT MIGRATIONS

minor conflicts have created new minority problems. For centuries the boundaries of states have depended upon the fortunes of war. Borders have been drawn almost entirely on the basis of political, economic and military considerations. The wishes and rights of peoples have been disregarded or flouted. Large numbers of men and women have been shunted back and forth between rulers and states as if they were chattels. In certain cases, notably Poland, whole nations have been partitioned among great powers.

Now since the dawn of history tyrannical majority peoples have persecuted the minorities that lived within the territory under the majority population's control. These majorities have often tried to destroy the minorities' national, cultural and religious consciousness. Unfortunately, this kind of persecution is still going on even in our own age.

In the Middle Ages, and in early modern times, when the peoples of Western Europe were united in one Church, and religious differences were not tolerated, it was the religious minorities which were persecuted. During the nineteenth century, however, when the spirit of modern nationalism arose, the problem of national and cultural minorities came to the fore. In the name of national self-determination, Germans, Hungarians and Italians demanded and secured freedom from alien rule, both politically and culturally.

Soon, however, smaller or weaker groups living among the Germans and Hungarians were seized by the same feeling of nationalism and made similar demands for political and cultural autonomy. To this demand the dominant peoples turned a deaf ear. They were so convinced of the excellence of their own government and culture that they considered it a boon to the "less advanced" peoples to be "Germanized" or "Magyarized" or "Russified," etc.

THE ASSIMILATION OF ALIEN PEOPLES

In some cases minorities have been assimilated in this way. But for the most part attempts at compulsory assimilation of smaller or weaker groups have not been successful. In spite of persecutions, in spite of economic and political handicaps, in spite of the penalty of inferior social status, the minorities have usually clung to their own national, cultural or religious ideas and loyalties.

III. The Minorities Before the World War

In the Europe that existed before the World War, millions of minority peoples were unwilling subjects of the three great empires of Germany, Austria-Hungary and Russia (see the map on page 17). For many years before the outbreak of the war, Europe was preoccupied with the gigantic struggle between two rival groups of imperialist states, particularly the fierce clash between Germany and Russia. Allied with Germany against Russia in the contest that was being waged from Persia through the Near East, the Balkans, and the Danube and Baltic areas, was Austria-Hungary.

PAN-SLAVISM

In those days Pan-Slavism was a terrifying word to many Germans, Austrians and Hungarians. Pan-Slavism was a movement to unite all the Slavs of Europe. It meant the threat of an alliance of all the Slavic peoples in a great world force. To the Austrians and Hungarians it also meant the possible destruction of their Dual Monarchy. For within the Hapsburg empire were incorporated millions of Czechs, Slovaks, Poles, Slovenes, Serbs, Croats (pronounced *crow*-ats) and Ruthenes. Nearly all of these non-German and non-Magyar peoples wanted cultural or political autonomy; some demanded outright independence. In their political aspirations they were encouraged by the Russian Empire.

But Pan-Slavism never developed much farther than the academic stage. True, the Pan-Slavic dream had enormous possibilities. A confederation that could have united all the Slavic tribes would have brought together almost two hundred million people under the Pan-Slavic banner. It would have offered a serious, perhaps an overwhelming, challenge to Pan-Germanism—a similar movement to unite all the Germans in Europe.

But the fatal weakness of Pan-Slavism was the fact that the

various branches of the great Slavic family considered themselves Poles, or Czechs, or Serbs rather than members of one all-inclusive nation. Consequently, even while the Pan-Slavic agitation continued, the Poles in Russia were waging an unceasing struggle to win their freedom from the Slavic empire of which they were unwilling subjects.

THE WAR GIVES MINORITIES THEIR CHANCE

The outbreak of the World War did not put an end to this minority struggle in Russia and other belligerent states. On the contrary, the war gave the minorities an opportunity to renew their efforts to win national and cultural freedom. While Polish, Czech, French, Rumanian, Serbian and other minorities were drafted by their governments for service at the front, their relatives at home and abroad, in most cases, were carrying on unceasing campaigns against the respective régimes which ruled them.

MINORITIES ESTABLISH GOVERNMENTS DURING WAR

While the war was still being bitterly fought on its various fronts, some of the minorities were already establishing governments of their own. Thus we find that even before the Allies' victory the Czechs and the Slovaks had launched a movement for national freedom. The Poles likewise were preparing for the day when they could triumphantly establish their independent homeland. Minorities of Serbs, Rumanians, Lithuanians, Italians, Danes and other peoples were looking forward to reunion with their brethren.

This minorities agitation undoubtedly hastened the collapse of the Austro-Hungarian monarchy, and thereby shortened the war. Allied propaganda was able to encourage these independence movements among the minorities in Germany and Austria-Hungary. But some of the Allied promises made to minority peoples in 1918 were to cause trouble later on.

THE MINORITIES IN EUROPE'S PRE-WAR EMPIRES

THE PRINCIPLE OF SELF-DETERMINATION

Before the Armistice President Wilson had championed the ideal of the "self-determination of peoples." The principle of self-determination means the right of each people to decide for itself what nation it wants to belong to. Wilson's idealism heartened millions of minority peoples living in Germany, Austria-Hungary and the Russian domains. This ideal of "self-determination" was nobly conceived. But it is an ideal which is impossible to carry out in full. For harassed Allied statesmen soon discovered that a settlement which suited one people usually met with the bitter opposition of one or more other peoples. It was one thing to promise an equitable settlement of the minorities problem; it was something else to carry out that promise.

THE MINORITIES QUESTION AT THE PEACE CONFERENCE

In January 1919, when the various delegations arrived in Paris to begin the Peace Conference, they were met by a multitude of official and unofficial representatives of the new states and the peoples who wanted to found new states. The demands and counter-demands of these small nations created a regular bedlam. To add to the confusion, there were sometimes rival delegations. In the case of the Russians, for instance, there were White Russian delegations at Paris, although Red Russians ruled most of Russia. There were also rival Ukrainian representatives who warred against each other and clamored for recognition of their claims.

Secret treaties written during the war now bobbed up to plague those who had signed them. Italy demanded that her allies recognize the Treaty of London, signed in 1915, which promised the Italians territories along the Adriatic. But in those territories only a minority of the population is Italian: the majority population is Slavic. How could the British and French turn over to Latin Italy a large population of South

Slavs without doing injustice to another of their allies, the Kingdom of Serbia? Yet when the British and French failed to make good their treaty promises to Italy, the flamboyant Italian poet Gabriele D'Annunzio and his legionaries seized the city of Fiume, an Adriatic port claimed by the new state of the Serbs, Croats and Slovenes (later called Yugoslavia) as its chief seaport (see the map in the center of the book).

While Italians and South Slavs quarreled bitterly over the eastern shore of the Adriatic, Lithuanians and Poles fought over the territory around Vilna. Lithuanians demanded that the Allies cede the former German city of Memel to them. Czechs and Poles came to blows over the district of Teschen. Warfare raged between Finns and Soviet Russians. Ukrainians fought against Soviet Russians, anti-Soviet Russians, Poles and Rumanians. Ruthenians and Hungarians clashed. Hungarians fought against Czechs. The Rumanians occupied the province of Bessarabia, held for a century by Russia, amid outraged protests from Russians, Soviet and anti-Soviet alike. And Greeks clamored for the annexation of Constantinople. (For all these places, see the center map.)

IMPOSSIBILITY OF SATISFYING ALL PEOPLES

When the Allied delegates got down to the task of drawing the new frontiers of Europe they soon learned that it was an utter impossibility to create frontiers that did not cut off some people from what should have been their home-state. The "islands" of different nationalities scattered across the continent made it absolutely out of the question to find any settlement that could unite all the minorities with their own brethren.

For an example of this problem, take Transylvania (map, p. 45). That former Austro-Hungarian province was claimed by the kingdom of Rumania, one of the victorious nations. But this colorful province is occupied by three peoples: Hungarians, Germans and Rumanians (map, p. 45). To make the situation even more complex, a heavy block of Rumanians lies next to the main block of the Hungarian population of Hungary. On the other side of Transylvania, not far from the borders of the old kingdom, there are four counties heavily populated with Hungarians. These Magyars live in practically the geographical center of Greater Rumania. Yet in Transylvania itself the majority of the people are Rumanians.

Here was a minorities problem to baffle any expert. For the mosaic of peoples in Transylvania is so intricately composed that no map-maker could draw frontiers that would not leave some people on the wrong side of the border line. And that was only one of several mixed nationality areas the Peace Conference had to consider.

INTERNATIONAL POLITICS TAKES A HAND

Unfortunately, the new frontiers were not always drawn with the purpose of carrying out the ideal of "self-determination" even when that was possible. This was particularly true in the case of the new frontiers of Hungary, which cut off blocks of Magyars from the bulk of the Hungarian population in the home-state (map, p. 43).

Worse still, some of the borders were drawn in defiance of economic common sense. An example was post-war Austria, a state which the new borders cut off from many areas on which it had formerly depended economically (map, p. 21). These lost areas had provided the Austrians with both raw materials and markets. So after the peace settlement Austria suffered great economic hardship.

The ideal of "self-determination" also had to give way in many cases to the rivalries of the great powers. A frontier that should have been drawn in the interest of the people living in that vicinity was sometimes dictated by the general staff of a state situated on the other side of Europe.

WHAT THE WORLD WAR DID TO THE MAP OF EUROPE

The minority problems would have been difficult enough in an atmosphere of peace and tolerance. They became much worse in the spirit of hatred, greed and extreme nationalism that ruled many of the representatives who met at Paris to negotiate a series of treaties to end the World War officially.

The states on the losing side—Germany, Austria-Hungary, Bulgaria and Turkey—had grounds for their charges that the peace treaties were dictated pacts. But several powers on the winning side were not satisfied either. Italy, for one, bitterly disapproved of certain parts of the treaties. Her territorial gains fell far short of her demands. Poland likewise was not satisfied. Nor were Lithuania and the Kingdom of the Serbs, Croats and Slovenes (Yugoslavia). Even in France there was criticism of the treaties on the ground that they did not go far enough toward preventing future German aggression. And there were leaders in France, like the late Marshal Foch, who advocated permanent French occupation of the west bank of the Rhine, even though that would have created a new German minority within the borders of France.

THE MINORITY DISPUTES CONTINUE

Whether better treaties than those negotiated in 1919 could have been written is beside the point in this discussion. Many minority problems were solved and others were rendered less acute. What we must keep in mind, however, is the fact that several small nations emerged or were reborn at the Peace Conference. New frontiers were drawn. Old neighbors became separated and new nations became neighbors. Some ancient causes of international friction remained, and many new ones were created.

Among the Slavs, for example, Russians and Poles continued their ancient feud; Czechs and Poles were at swords' points; and Serbs and Bulgars fought along their common border. Latin France and Teutonic Germany, glaring at each other across the Rhine, hated each other no more intensely than did post-war Slavic Czechs and Slavic Poles, arrayed against each other along their common frontier near Teschen. The Austrian German minority turned over to Italy by the Peace Conference protested no more loudly than did the Macedonian Bulgarian minority in the Kingdom of the Serbs, Croats and Slovenes (Yugoslavia). Nor were the relations between the Serbs and Croats serene either.

SOME GOOD ACCOMPLISHED BY PEACE PACTS

There is another side of the ledger, however. The peace treaties did bring about a certain measure of "self-determination." For we must not forget that these treaties liberated ten peoples who before the war lived under foreign rule. In the name of "self-determination" these peoples were able to establish governments independent of their former rulers. They are the Poles, Lithuanians, Czechs, Slovaks, Serbs, Croats, Slovenes, Finns, Estonians and Letts.

The treaties did, therefore, rectify some long-standing injustices. Moreover, they provided for plebiscites in certain disputed areas, notably in the Saar, in Silesia and in East Prussia (center map).

Furthermore, the treaties provided that some of the states governing minorities should give guarantees on behalf of their minority groups. These pacts promised that the majority governments would respect the language, religious and cultural rights of the minorities. Such guarantees were at least a step in the right direction. Unfortunately, they were imposed upon some governments but not on others. "Thus," writes Professor Janowsky, "provisions for the protection of minorities were incorporated in the peace treaties made with the smaller defeated states, namely Austria, Hungary, Bulgaria and Turkey," but not in that with Germany.

THE MINORITIES TREATIES

"More important," he continues, "were the special Minorities Treaties which the Allied and Associated Powers imposed upon the new or enlarged states of Poland, Czechoslovakia, Yugoslavia, Rumania and Greece. Several other states, such as Lithuania, Latvia and Estonia, were refused admission into the League of Nations until each had expressly committed itself in a Declaration, made before the Council of the League, to respect the rights of minorities. Finally, provision was made for minorities in a limited number of bilateral conventions [or treaties between two nations] in which the signatories mutually undertook to treat justly with their minorities."

NEW MIGRATIONS OF PEOPLES

The months that immediately followed the Peace Conference saw large movements of peoples throughout Central Europe, the Balkans, the Baltic region and Russia. Wherever one traveled in those areas he saw refugees in flight. It was not uncommon to see families living on top of freight cars, cooking, eating and sleeping on their precarious perch. Babies were born on these roofs while trains were in motion. Men and women died on them. Sometimes they were swept off by low overhead bridges.

Religious as well as national minorities were forced into flight by the new order. For it must be kept in mind that in many cases the new minorities were the old ruling groups, the former minority having become part of the new majority. So it was now their turn to apply the screw. In all too many instances the people who had only recently been oppressed now turned oppressors.

If you will turn to the map of Europe in the center of this book and mark a wide swath right down across the Continent from Finland to the Aegean Sea, you will see the area in which the greatest post-war movements of peoples took place. This was a kind of no-man's-land. Political frontiers were unstable. Wars were still in progress. Rival ideologies were struggling for control. Trade was only beginning to revive. And the wreckage of the World War was being cleared away slowly and laboriously. Only those who actually came into contact with the armies of refugees during this period can adequately appreciate the suffering of the minorities affected by the peace treaties and the aftermath of the great conflict.

IV. The Minorities After the World War: 1

In order to get a better understanding of the minorities problem, let us take a quick trip through the post-war states in which dissatisfied minorities live. Before we set out, though, perhaps we ought to make sure we know exactly what a minority is.

Some states—France, for instance—are relatively homogeneous in population, while other states comprise groups of peoples of widely differing ancestry. These "ethnic" groups are sometimes called nationalities, and the smaller or weaker of them are frequently called minorities. In this book we shall refer to them as minorities.

WHAT IS A MINORITY?

Is a minority a separate "race"? No, definitely not. There are *no* "pure" races in Europe. That is one of the few flat statements that can be made on the subject of minorities. Certain so-called "racial experts" of Nazi Germany talk as if some human "races" (especially the "Aryan") were "pure." But that is nonsense. There are no "pure" human stocks in Europe. What the German Nazis call "racial purity" is a myth. In application it is a dangerous myth. It cannot be supported on either historical or scientific grounds.

If a minority is not a separate race, what is it?

One of the leading authorities on the subject of minorities

has sanctioned the following definition: "A minority is a body of people bound together by a consciousness of kind, rooted in common ancestry, traditions, language, culture or religion, *which sets them off from the majority or dominant people in the country in which they live.*"

COMPACT AND DISPERSED MINORITIES

Frequently minorities are to be found along the borders of a state. If this borderland adjoins another state in which the minority people forms the majority, a partial solution of the minority problem might perhaps be found in territorial "adjustments." But numerous minorities live in "islands," or "enclaves," entirely surrounded by other peoples, and distant from their own kinsmen. For such peoples obviously no territorial settlement could be satisfactory. The only possible solution of the problem of such minorities is some kind of arrangement guaranteeing them the right to preserve their own language and traditions and equal civil rights with the majority people. The same is true of minority peoples who are so interspersed among the majority that it would be practically impossible for them to govern themselves as a unit.

With these general principles in mind, let us begin our trip. We might start with Germany—the largest of the defeated nations.

MINORITIES IN THE GERMAN REPUBLIC

In visiting post-war Germany we ought to keep in mind the fact that the pre-war German monarchy had been swept away and was replaced by a liberal government. The militarists were out of power; the pacifists were in. The German Republic that was set up in 1919 was governed by Socialists, Catholics and other groups which had been discriminated against at one time or another in the past. The new government sin-

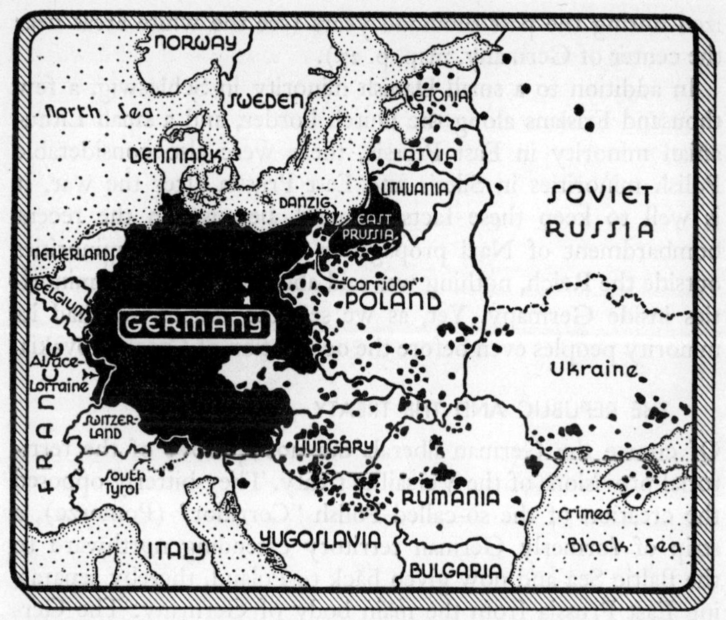

THE GERMANS IN EUROPE

cerely wanted peace and the opportunity to recover from the long, terrible years of war.

Now the German liberals, it should be emphasized, adopted a more tolerant attitude toward the minorities in the Republic than had the rulers of Imperial Germany. The founders of the German Republic did not indulge in theories of "racial superiority." They knew that large numbers of the German people had Slavic ancestors. They knew that this was especially true of the Prussians, who are believed to be a mixture of Slavic and Teutonic speaking peoples both of whom had probably intermarried with Lithuanians and other tribes.

German liberals knew that the Polabs, for example, were Slavs of the Elbe valley who had gradually become Germanized during the past thousand years (see the white areas near the center of Germany, map, p. 27).

In addition to a small Danish minority in Schleswig, a few thousand Frisians along the Dutch border, and a small Lithuanian minority in East Prussia, there were also considerable Polish minorities in Silesia and East Prussia after the war. It is well to keep these facts in mind, because, in the recent bombardment of Nazi propaganda about German minorities outside the Reich, nothing was said about non-German minorities inside Germany. Yet, as we see, the Reich, too, had its minority peoples even before the occupation of Czechoslovakia.

THE REPUBLIC AND THE TREATY

Of course the German liberals did not approve of the territorial provisions of the Versailles treaty. They bitterly opposed the creation of the so-called Polish "Corridor" (Pomorze), a strip of formerly German territory extending northward to the Baltic Sea and now given back to Poland, thereby separating East Prussia from the main body of Germany. The German Republic contested Polish claims to regions in Upper Silesia and around Posen. They protested the establishment of the Free City of Danzig. And they demanded that Memel remain part of Germany. (You will find all of these disputed territories marked on the map in the center of the book.)

In other words, the German liberals were patriotic Germans looking after their country's territorial interests. They were not, as Hitler has charged, a group of traitors. But they did not champion Pan-Germanism or the *Drang nach Osten* (drive to the East), although they favored the union of Germany and Austria.

In fact, one of the hopes of the German Republic was to bring about a merger of these two German-speaking countries. German and Austrian liberals advocated *Anschluss* (union) not only for sentimental reasons but for economic reasons as well. But the Allies would permit no move toward such a union. Even the formation of a customs union between these two Germanic states was prohibited.

This Allied opposition to the union of liberal Germany and liberal Austria seems bitterly ironic in the light of what was to follow less than two decades later. For in March 1938, without so much as a "please" to the League or anybody else, Hitler marched his German legions into Austria and annexed it to the Third Reich. In taking this action he claimed that he was merely reuniting the Austrian Germans with their blood-brothers in Germany. And Field Marshal Goering asserted that in occupying Austria Germany was protecting the Germans in Austria from the "bludgeons" of their "tormentors." He did not explain who these tormentors were, but he did say frankly that "the German Reich considers itself as in every respect the protector and patron of all Germans, including those outside the frontiers."

In a moment we shall see how this doctrine was subsequently used to dismember Czechoslovakia.

MINORITIES IN THE BALTIC NATIONS

Now turn to the map on page 31 and you will see the eastern Baltic states with their minorities represented by different shadings. In addition to those actually shown there are some small dispersed minorities in these states, namely a few Letts along the border and Jews in the towns of Estonia, a number of Poles, Jews and Lithuanians in Latvia, and some scattered Letts, Russians and White Russians in Lithuania.

But the most important minority in these countries from our point of view is the German. The Germans in Estonia and Latvia are descendants of the Teutonic Knights and traders who once ruled this region and they have therefore a tradition of superiority.

LITHUANIA

At the Peace Conference, the Lithuanians claimed not only the present territory of Lithuania proper but also the city of Vilna and its hinterland. Moreover, they laid claim to the Memel region (center map). These claims brought the Lithuanians into conflict with two vastly larger states, Poland and Germany. For Poland also claimed Vilna, and Germany refused to recognize the Lithuanian claims to Memel.

THE DISPUTE ABOUT VILNA

Early post-war Lithuanian, Soviet and Polish efforts to control Vilna are too complicated to be treated here in detail. But in October 1920 a Polish army of irregulars drove the Lithuanian forces out of Vilna and took possession of that ancient city in the name of Poland. The Lithuanians, in a counter-action, immediately closed their frontier with Poland. For seventeen and a half years thereafter, no train, automobile or carriage crossed that sealed frontier. Telephone and telegraph wires were cut. Mail between Lithuania and Poland that should have crossed this border had to be routed through Germany or Latvia. Lithuanians and Poles no longer spoke to each other. Finally, in March 1938, by threatening immediate invasion if her ultimatum were not obeyed, Poland succeeded in forcing Lithuania to reopen the border and restore normal relations.

What is the truth about these conflicting claims to Vilna? Both Lithuania and Poland can claim "historic" rights to the disputed city. And it must be remembered that the Poles and Lithuanians were united under one government for many years. The Vilna district has a mixed population, but most experts seem to believe that the city of Vilna itself is predominantly Polish. The region surrounding the city, however, contains many White Russians and Lithuanians. So in this area of

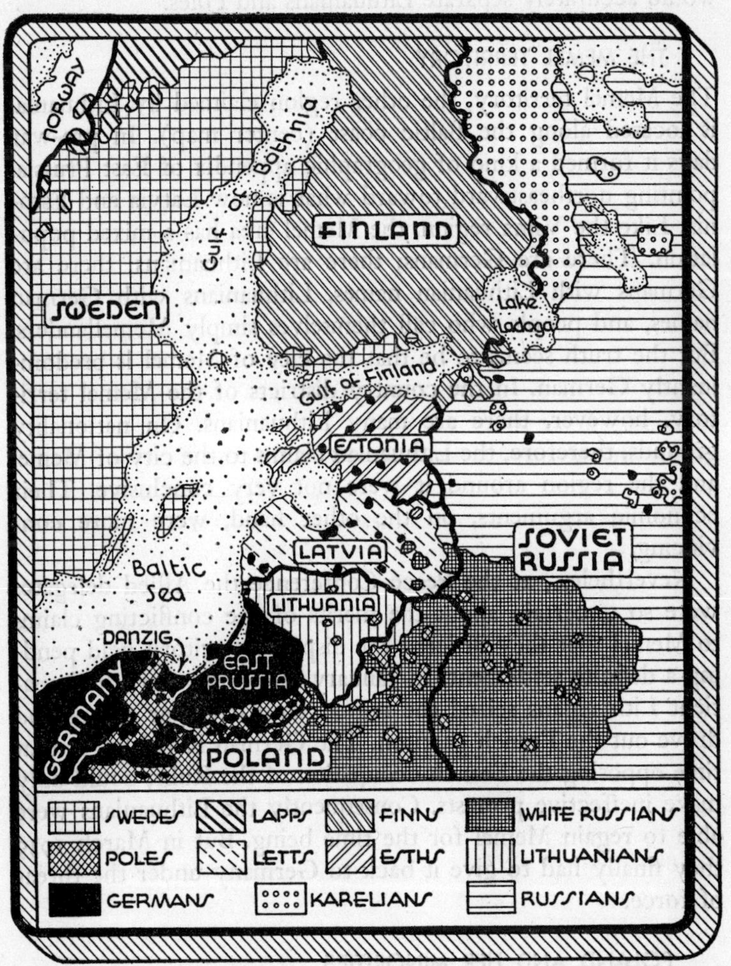

THE PEOPLES OF THE BALTIC STATES

mixed nationalities it would be impossible to draw a line that would accurately separate Lithuanians and Poles.

THE MEMEL TERRITORY

The Memel territory, the other region claimed by Lithuania, is located along the Baltic coast (center map). In pre-war days it formed a kind of geographic appendix of East Prussia, pointing northeastward toward what is now Latvia and Estonia. Like the Vilna region, the Memel area has a mixed population. There are Germans; there are Lithuanians; there are Germans with Lithuanian names, Lithuanians with German names, and people who call themselves simply Memellanders. But the truth seems to be that the city of Memel is predominantly German. In the country districts of the Memel territory, however, there are many Lithuanians. On nationality grounds, therefore, the Lithuanian claims to the city of Memel and the region around it were not very conclusive. Their economic arguments, on the other hand, were more convincing.

Nevertheless, at the Peace Conference the Allied delegates were so uncertain about the merits of the conflicting claims to Memel that they ordered the disputed territory held pending a definite settlement. In January 1923, however, the impatient Lithuanians seized the region with irregular troops and drove out the French garrison. The German Republic, at that time opposing the French occupation of the Ruhr, could only make ineffective protests. Consequently the Lithuanians were able to regain Memel for the time being. But in March 1939 they finally had to give it back to Germany under the threat of force.

POLAND AND HER MINORITIES

As we enter Poland (map, p. 35), we come into a state which had begun to rank as a near great power before Germany launched her invasion. In the matter of size it stands sixth in Europe. In population it ranks fifth on the Continent. Outside of Russia it has more minorities than any other European country. For these reasons alone Poland has an important place in our review of the minorities situation.

THE UKRAINIAN MINORITY IN POLAND

Poland's largest minority is Ukrainian. When we look at the map we see that the shading denoting the Ukrainians is spread over a large area that extends from the Rumanian and Hungarian frontiers northward to the Pripet river (map, p. 35). It stretches westward toward the central part of Poland. In this territory there is, however, a considerable Polish population. In other words, there is a Polish minority located within the area of the Ukrainian minority. Cities in this region, such as Lwow, are predominantly Polish and Jewish. And it should be noted that there are other minorities in this Ukrainian region also.

In such an interweaving of peoples, how would it be possible to draw a frontier that would leave Ukrainians on one side and Poles on the other? It would be impossible, of course. Nor is the situation rendered any simpler by the fact that the shading which indicates the Ukrainian minority splashes over the frontiers of Hungary and Rumania and forms a broad expanse over in the Soviet Union (map, p. 91).

Poland's second largest minority is the Jewish minority. The Jews in Poland are scattered all over the country. They number about 3,000,000. They are concentrated mainly in the cities, and to a considerable extent they are engaged in trade. The growth of a Polish middle class, of cooperatives, and of economic nationalism has resulted in an effort to encourage the economic activities of the majority population at the expense of the Jews. The more reckless elements in the population have organized boycotts and fomented riots. At times even the government has not been unsympathetic to the anti-Jewish agitation, especially in its economic aspect.

THE WHITE RUSSIAN MINORITY IN POLAND

North of the Ukrainian area in Poland we see the shadings for Poles, White Russians and Lithuanians (map, p. 35). There are also, in the southwest, a few border communities of Czechs—too tiny to show—and along the Soviet border some scattered Great Russians. The shaded area which represents the White Russians overflows across Poland's eastern frontier into the Soviet Union. But throughout this region where the White Russians live there are districts inhabited by overwhelmingly Polish populations. Again we see a territory in which it would be impossible to draw a frontier separating one people from another.

THE GERMAN MINORITY IN POLAND

The fourth largest minority in Poland is German. When the map-makers at the Peace Conference attempted to draw a frontier between Poles and Germans they found that it would be an impossible task. Thus along much of the Polish-German frontier the respective shadings denoting these peoples do not stop at the boundary line (map, p. 35). At one point the German shading runs into Poland. At another the Polish shading runs into Germany. We note that the black, which stands for Germans, is most evident in the regions that were formerly part of the Reich—that is, in the Polish Corridor, around Posen and in Polish (Upper) Silesia.

THE POLISH CORRIDOR (POMORZE)

For centuries the Polish Corridor region has been a battle-ground between German and Pole. It has been held at one time or another by both peoples. The consequence is that

THE MAJORITY AND MINORITY PEOPLES OF POLAND

today its population is a mixed one, although impartial records favor the Poles' claim that they heavily outnumber the Germans in the Corridor. This strip of land, which gave Poland access to the sea, cut the Reich in two and thereby caused Germany some understandable inconvenience. Poland's right of access to the sea was recognized by the thirteenth of President Wilson's Fourteen Points. And even though East Prussia was separated by the Corridor from the main body of the Reich, the two parts of Germany did have access to each other by sea and by rail.

But for Poland it was a matter of life and death to hold on to the Corridor, for the Corridor was Poland's only outlet to the Baltic Sea and the outside world. Consequently when Germany demanded a corridor through the Corridor, Poland refused. And when Germany threatened to use force to gain her demands, the Poles still refused. So we see in the Corridor region today a struggle in progress that has been going on for at least six centuries.

V. The Minorities After the World War: 2

The emergence of the Czechoslovak state even before the end of the World War was another triumph of historic justice. For three centuries the Czechs had been living in lands ruled by the Hapsburgs. The World War brought about the break-up of the Hapsburg Empire and the liberation of the Czechs from Austria and the Slovaks from Hungary.

MINORITIES IN CZECHOSLOVAKIA

But the boundaries of the new Czechoslovak state that were drawn at the Peace Conference were far from being nationality frontiers. These borders were drawn for other reasons: economic, military and political. We need only point out that these frontiers incorporated within the borders of Czechoslovakia millions of minority peoples. There were more than three million Germans, about 700,000 Magyars, nearly a half million Ukrainians (Ruthenians) and smaller minorities of Jews, Poles and Rumanians (map, p. 39).

THE SUDETEN GERMANS

Now very few of the German inhabitants of Czechoslovakia had ever lived inside Germany. For nearly all the "Sudetens," as they are called, were not Reich Germans but Germans of Austria. But the Slovaks, Magyars and Ukrainians of Czechoslovakia had been citizens of Hungary. Furthermore, the Magyar minority was, in the main, compactly located along the northern frontier of the Hungarian motherland. In these circumstances it would have been strange if the Hungarians had not protested against a settlement which, they charged, violated the promise of "self-determination."

The Polish minority in the Teschen district (map, p. 39), though small, immediately became a bone of contention between Czechs and Poles. Poland laid claim to the district. The Czechoslovaks, on the other hand, were adamant in their determination to hold it. On the map the Teschen district seems insignificant. Yet it prevented friendly cooperation between Poles and Czechoslovaks.

Although the minorities in Czechoslovakia undoubtedly had numerous causes for complaint, it is only fair to add that this Central European "island of democracy" treated its minorities more generously than did any other new state in central Europe. Czechoslovakia's minority policies were enlightened and fundamentally sound.

THE DISMEMBERMENT OF CZECHOSLOVAKIA

Nevertheless, that fact did not prevent Hitler from using the German minority to dismember and destroy that little state. By claiming that the Sudeten Germans were being persecuted by the Czechs, demanding their incorporation in the Reich in accordance with the principle of self-determination, and threatening to plunge Europe into war if he did not get his way, he succeeded in persuading the governments of Great Britain, France and Italy to cooperate with him in compelling the Czechs to cede the German areas of Czechoslovakia to Germany. The agreement was reached at a conference held at Munich in September 1938 and was immediately carried out. At the same time Poland got the Teschen district and Hungary occupied the areas inhabited by Magyars (map, p. 39).

In a conversation with Prime Minister Chamberlain of Great Britain a few days before the Munich conference, Hitler had said that the Sudetenland was his last territorial ambition in Europe. But less than six months later, on the pretext that the Germans living in what was left of Czechoslovakia were being brutally treated, he invaded the provinces of Bohemia, Moravia and Slovakia and made them "protectorates" of the Reich. Simultaneously Hungary annexed Ruthenia, the easternmost province of Czechoslovakia and the only part that was left

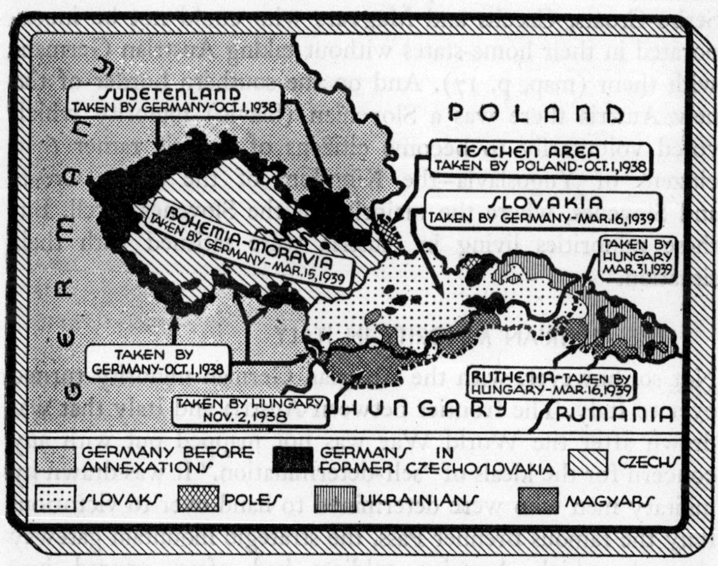

THE PEOPLES OF CZECHOSLOVAKIA, AND WHAT HAPPENED TO THEM

after Hitler's annexations (map, above). Thus Hitler added millions of non-Germans to his territories and Hungary acquired a large Ukrainian minority. Thus, too, the only country in Central Europe which had even tried to treat all its minorities fairly disappeared from the map.

MINORITIES IN THE NEW AUSTRIA

Crossing the Czechoslovak frontier into Austria, we also find minority problems, but on a quite different basis. For Austria was one of the nations that lost the war. Her chief minority troubles were outside her borders. In other words, the new frontiers that were drawn for Austria at the Peace Conference left numerous German-speaking Austrians *outside* Austria.

True, there were in pre-war Austria small minorities of Serbo-Croats, Czechs and Magyars who could not be incorporated in their home-states without taking Austrian Germans with them (map, p. 17). And on the southern border of the new Austria there was a Slovenian (Slavic) minority which voted voluntarily to become citizens of Austria rather than citizens of Yugoslavia—the Kingdom of the Serbs, Croats and Slovenes, where the majority of the Slovenes dwell. But these minorities living in Austria were satisfied with their situation.

THE AUSTRIAN MINORITY IN ITALY

Not so, however, with the Austrian German minority turned over to Italy. The frontier between Austria and Italy that was drawn after the World War was not mapped out with any concern for the ideals of "self-determination." It was drawn by military men who were determined to hand over to victorious Italy the famous Brenner Pass, the strategic mountain gateway through which Austrian soldiers had often poured into Italian lands.

It would have been impossible, in any case, to give Italy the region on the south side of the Brenner without turning over nearly a quarter of a million Austrian Germans to the Italians. But to make matters worse, Italy set to work to transform these Germans into Italians. The Italian campaign to bring this about was at once harsh and thorough. Consequently Europe heard many protests from the Austrian Germans in Italy and from their brothers in the Austrian homeland and throughout Germany. When we come to consider Italy's minority problems we shall see what eventually happened to the Austrian minority in Italy.

When we cross the Austrian border into Hungary, the land of the Magyars, we find a people who differ in many ways from the Germans, Slavs or Latins. Their only relatives in Europe are the Estonians and Finns, located far away.

In pre-war Hungary there were millions of minority peoples: Germans, Slovaks, Serbs, Croats, Slovenes, Rumanians, Gypsies and others (map, p. 17). Many of the minority peoples of pre-war Hungary were not contented. They wanted to be included in the countries of their kin, if they existed, or to have countries made for them, if they didn't.

Hungary's defeat in the World War gave these minorities their chance to break away from Hungarian rule. After the war the old Hungary was cut into six pieces (map, p. 21). The largest was the new kingless "kingdom" of Hungary; other slices went to Rumania, Czechoslovakia and Yugoslavia. One tiny area that included Fiume went to Italy. Another went by plebiscite to Austria. Each of these shifts of territory linked to their home-state a minority people who had formerly been living in Hungary. But along with these people went a lot of Hungarians–nearly three millions of them, to be exact. These Hungarians were now, against their will, included in Czechoslovakia, Rumania and Yugoslavia (map, p. 43).

Consequently the new borders created bitter opposition in Hungary. From the great landed aristocrat down to the simple peasant working in the fields, Magyars without exception opposed this dictated settlement. Budapest rang with denunciation of the treaty and with appeals to the Allied nations to rectify the pact, which Magyars sincerely believed was a triumph of wrong over right.

In the years after the war the Hungarians would show you a photograph of a house divided by the new frontiers–one half in Hungary, the other half in Rumania. They would show you the picture of a Magyar peasant whose home was still in Hungary but whose fields were in Czechoslovakia. They would tell you countless stories of persecution, of economic losses, of the denial of "self-determination"—all consequences of the hated peace settlement.

Much of this resentment against the treaty settlement was unjustified. For the various peoples of the old Hungary were so inextricably intermingled that no one could have drawn borders which would have included the chief minority groups in their home-states without taking a lot of Hungarians along with them.

We have already seen (p. 19) how impossible it was to draw a frontier separating Magyars from Rumanians in Transylvania. The same sort of thing is true of the Bachka district of Yugoslavia (map, p. 51). Here Magyars, Serbs and other peoples are woven into an intricate mosaic of nationalities. Now just suppose we tried to draw a nationality frontier through this district. As you can see from the maps, it would be impossible to trace a line that would give Hungary the Magyar minority without at the same time turning over to the Hungarians the city of Subotica, with its large Yugoslav population. So here again we come up against the hopeless task of drawing a frontier based upon the ideal of "self-determination." Obviously, any line which satisfied one people would draw instant protests from another.

NON-MAGYAR PEOPLES IN HUNGARY

There is another side to this Hungarian minority problem, too. The Hungarians' case against their new borders would be stronger if the new and smaller Hungary contained only Hungarians. But is post-war Hungary a one-people state occupied entirely by Magyars? By no means. Even after the narrowed post-war frontiers were drawn, there still remained in Hungary about a half million Germans and much

THE HUNGARIANS AND THE MINORITIES IN HUNGARY

smaller minorities of Slovaks, Serbs, Rumanians, Slovenes and Jews (map, above). With the seizure of Ruthenia, the easternmost province of Czechoslovakia, as well as parts of Slovakia, in March 1939, Hungary has now acquired also a considerable Ukrainian minority and has added to the numbers of her Slovak minority.

But if the Hungarians' resentment against their post-war borders is not entirely justified, it is nevertheless very strong. And before the outbreak of the present war it was a source of considerable danger, too. In fact, the Hungarian minority problem was regarded by informed observers as a serious threat to European peace, especially as it seemed to be regarded by Italy as a means of stirring up internal troubles in Yugoslavia that would keep that country from taking a strong stand against Italy in international affairs.

RUMANIA AND HER MINORITIES

Let us look now at the situation in the kingdom of Rumania.

Even before the World War Rumania had her minorities of Bulgarians, Jews, Turks and Tartars. The peace treaties gave this kingdom large tracts of territory that formerly belonged to Austria-Hungary (map, p. 21). The Rumanians also occupied the province of Bessarabia (center map), land that had been part of the pre-war Russian Empire. With these new territories Rumania added to her population millions of Magyars, Jews, Germans, Poles, Russians, Ukrainians, Serbs, Slovaks and members of other minorities (map, p. 45).

So it is that even though Rumania's territory was virtually doubled as a result of the peace treaties, her position in Europe was not necessarily made more secure. The Soviet Union, for instance, refused to recognize the Rumanian annexation of Bessarabia. Nor did the Hungarians accept as final the treaty which gave Rumania Transylvania and part of the Banat. And all the time Bulgaria fiercely resented her new frontier with Rumania, for it separated a sizable Bulgarian minority from the motherland.

Later on, we shall see how other nations are using this minorities situation to interfere in Rumanian internal affairs and to threaten the kingdom's existence.

THE RUMANIANS AND THEIR MINORITIES

BULGARIA AND HER MINORITIES

If we board a train in Bucharest, the Rumanian capital, and travel a few miles south, we arrive at the town of Giurgiu on the north bank of the Danube (center map). There we take a steamer to cross to Bulgaria. Though Bulgaria was one of the losers in the World War and was shorn of territory by the

Treaty of Neuilly, she still retains minorities which total more than three quarters of a million (map, p. 53). But we are not primarily interested in the national minorities within Bulgaria. They are not a threat to peace. It is the Bulgarian minorities in other countries that we must study, because they represent an explosive factor in Balkan—and hence in European—affairs.

THE BULGARIANS OUTSIDE BULGARIA

On the map on page 53 you notice that the shading denoting the Bulgarians runs across the Bulgarian frontiers into Rumania, Yugoslavia, Greece and Turkey.

Bulgaria's chief minority dispute after the war was with Yugoslavia. For years after the World War the border between Bulgaria and Yugoslavia was the scene of violence, indeed, of pitched battles. This frontier bristled with barbed wire and machine guns and was said to have been strewn with wolf traps set for men.

THE MACEDONIANS

The cause of this unusual situation was the Macedonians. Their home is that rather barren region that is now included in southern Yugoslavia and northern Greece (map, p. 53). The origin of the Macedonians is a matter of dispute between Serbs and Bulgars. It seems probable that the Macedonians are related to both these peoples. Anyway, after the war Macedonians who lived within the borders of Bulgaria made repeated raids into Yugoslavia, then retreated from the Yugoslav soldiers and police into Bulgaria.

Bulgarians tell us that there can be no real peace and good will in the Balkans until the map is redrawn so that the Bulgarian minorities just outside the borders of the home-state (including the Bulgarian Macedonians) are reunited with their Bulgarian brothers. To do this, however, it would be necessary to take land away from the four members of the Balkan Entente. And these states refuse to make territorial concessions to Bulgaria.

In reply to them the Bulgarians quote Byron's line: "For time at last sets all things even." They have waited before, they tell you, and they can wait again. And so the Bulgarians are waiting for the next turn of the wheel of destiny, hoping that it may give them their opportunity to change the map of the Balkans. But while they are waiting, their neighbors are uneasy. And the Balkans cannot settle down to a tranquil existence as long as Bulgaria continues to harbor such hopes.

YUGOSLAVIA AND HER MINORITIES

Moving westward from Bulgaria we enter the kingdom of Yugoslavia. Created after the World War by enlarging the pre-war country of Serbia (map, p. 21), Yugoslavia was formerly called the Kingdom of the Serbs, Croats and Slovenes. The word Yugoslavia means the land of the South Slavs. The term South Slav is used to set the inhabitants of Yugoslavia off from the north Slavs—the Poles and Russians.

Our map of Yugoslavia shows a hodge-podge of shadings (map, p. 51). We find not only Serbs, Croats and Slovenes but also Germans, Rumanians, Macedonians, Bulgarians, Albanians and Hungarians (Magyars). There are also a few scattered Italians and Slovaks and a small Jewish minority. Moreover, about ten per cent of the people of Yugoslavia are of the Moslem faith. Most of these Mohammedans are Slavs whose ancestors adopted the religion of their Turkish masters several centuries ago.

The history of the minorities in Yugoslavia is not a tranquil one. For religious and cultural differences have often lined up one group against another. It is only fair to say, however, that these minority troubles have been intensified by agitation from without, especially from Italy and Hungary, and now

GENERAL REFERENCE MAP, SHOWING A

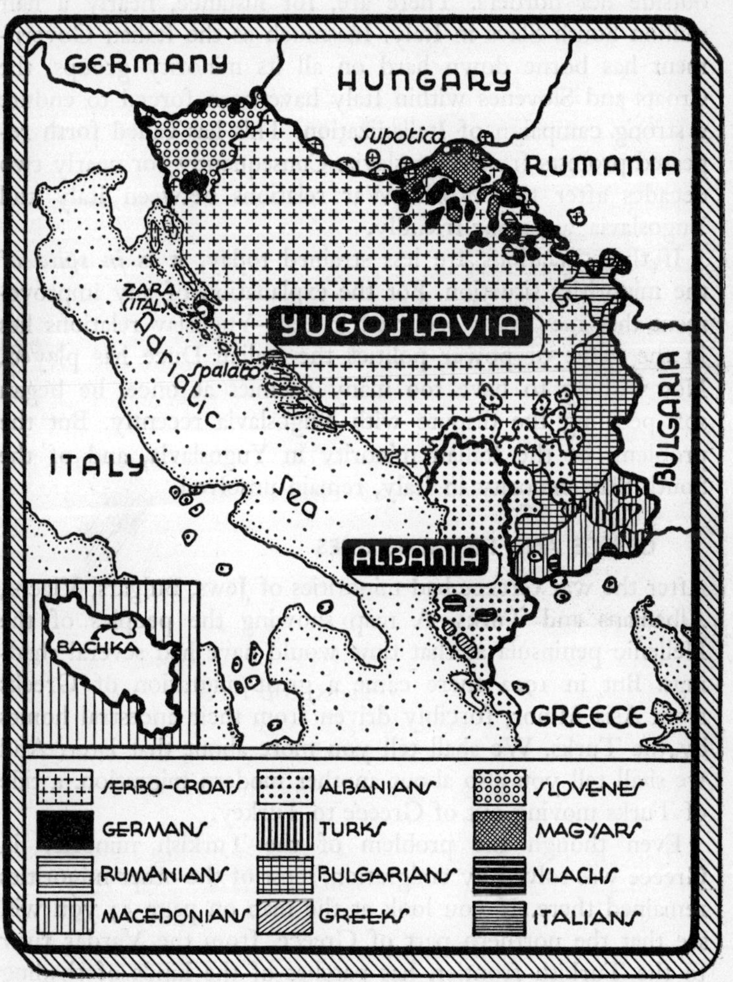

YUGOSLAVIA AND ALBANIA AND THEIR MINORITIES

Besides all these, Yugoslavia also has minority problems outside her borders. There are, for instance, nearly a half million South Slavs in Italy. Inasmuch as the Italian Government has borne down hard on all its minority groups, the Croats and Slovenes within Italy have been forced to endure a strong campaign of Italianization. This has called forth repeated protests from Yugoslavia. Consequently for nearly two decades after the World War relations between Italy and Yugoslavia were not friendly.

If those relations are less strained today, it is *in spite of* the minorities situation. For the explanation of any improvement that may have occurred in Italo-Yugoslav relations lies in the game of power politics the Italian Duce has played. Not wishing to have too many enemies at once, he began soft-pedaling the dispute with Yugoslavia recently. But the problems of the Italian minority in Yugoslavia, and of the South Slav minority in Italy, remain unsolved.

GREECE AND HER MINORITIES

After the war Greece had minorities of Jews, Bulgars, Vlachs, Albanians and Turks. A map showing the peoples of the Hellenic peninsula at that time would have had several shadings. But in 1922 there came a great migration of Greeks from Asia Minor, forcibly driven from their ancestral homes by the Turks. We shall tell you more about that later. And we shall tell you also about another modern migration, a tide of Turks moving out of Greece to Turkey.

Even though the problem of the Turkish minority in Greece was solved by emigration, most of the other minorities remained there. If you look at the map on page 53 you will see that the northern part of Greece, from the Vardar river to the Turkish frontier, has patches of the kinds of shading that stand for Bulgarians and Macedonians. Bulgaria claims much of this region not only on the basis of "self-determina-

MINORITY AND MAJORITY PEOPLES IN GREECE, BULGARIA AND TURKEY

tion" but also because she owned it for a short time between wars.

Greece is not uneasy about her Albanian minority, nor is she concerned about the Vlachs. With the Bulgarians and Macedonians, however, it is a different matter. These Slavic groups in Greece represent a constant source of irritation between the government of Greece and the government of Bulgaria. Here is a situation that presents a threat to peace in that part of Europe.

TURKEY IN EUROPE

Now if we cross the Maritza river we arrive in what remains of European Turkey (map, p. 53). Once the Turkish Empire stretched northward almost to Vienna. But now the main body of Turkey lies across the Sea of Marmora in Asia Minor. Turkey in Europe is only an outpost of the Turkish Republic.

It is an important outpost, however, and includes the ancient cities of Edirne, or Adrianople, and Istambul, or Constantinople (center map). Within Turkey in Europe there are several minorities. The most important are the Greeks, Jews and Bulgarians. Of these, the Bulgarians represent the most pressing minority problem of Turkey in Europe. That is because these Bulgars are located near the frontier of their national homeland, where there is a powerful sentiment in favor of incorporating them into Bulgaria.

The Bulgarians make the claim that if "self-determination" were actually put into effect a large slice of Turkey in Europe would go to Bulgaria. Needless to say, the Turks turn a deaf ear to this claim. The consequence is that there remains a grave minority dispute between Bulgaria and Turkey. As these lines are written, that feud is quiet. But any shift of the political balance in Europe could revive the Bulgarian-Turkish conflict.

VI. The Minorities After the World War: 3

We have come a long way since we set out on our tour of Europe at the beginning of Chapter IV. We have visited countries from Finland in the north of Europe to Turkey in the extreme southeast corner. Now let's swing north again, into the vast territories of the Soviet Union.

MINORITIES IN THE SOVIET UNION

In the days of the Russian Tsars, the Russians were the dominant folk in a land of many peoples. The frontiers that were finally drawn about the Soviet Union after the World War left outside tens of millions of Poles, Finns, Estonians, Letts, Lithuanians, White Russians, Ukrainians, Rumanians and others. But even after this drastic purge of non-Russian peoples from the Soviet Union, there still remained millions of non-Russians (see frontispiece map). If we consider the White Russians and Ukrainians as minorities, then we start with about forty million people. There are also millions of Tartars, Kirghiz, Bashkirs, Samoyedes, Mordvas, Kalmuks and other groups. Then there are national minorities of Germans, Poles, Finns, Turks, Rumanians, Greeks and others. A map showing the various peoples of Russia is an amazing patchwork.

When the Tsars ruled this vast territory, the non-Russians were not treated as equals. Their rights were restricted, their languages were forbidden, and they were not allowed to live in some parts of the country. So the lot of the minority peoples in Imperial Russia was not a happy one. The government made every effort to Russify these men and women whose speech, customs, religion and dress were non-Russian. But the Tsars were never very successful in their attempts to turn non-Russians into Muscovites.

When the Soviet Government came into power in 1917, minorities were for the first time recognized as the equals of the Russians. No longer did the slant-eyed Kirghiz from the steppes east of the Volga have to occupy an inferior position. Nor did the members of any other minority. The various minority peoples were now free to use their own languages. Furthermore many minorities were allowed to set up autonomous republics within the Union. And a new program of public welfare and education, some phases of which were planned especially to encourage the development of minority cultures, was set in motion.

Among the minorities, however, as in all other sectors of the Soviet population, there are dissident groups not sympathetic to the principles of communism. The point to notice is that the grievances of these groups are not the grievances of oppressed national minorities, but something entirely different.

Nevertheless, some people believe that the Soviet Union may be approaching the time when its national minorities will display the same symptoms of discontent that we find in Rumania, Poland, Lithuania and Yugoslavia. For some of the Soviet Union's national minorities may be reached by the propaganda of other nations. This applies especially to the Germans and the Ukrainians in the Union. We shall return to this subject later on.

ITALY AND HER MINORITIES

Out of forty-two million people in Italy, fewer than a million belong to national minorities (frontispiece map). So we think of Italy as a homogeneous state. But even though they are few in numbers, Italy's minorities are potentially dangerous to her. This is because her two largest minorities, the Germans and the South Slavs, are located along the frontiers of their respective homelands. And those homelands happen to be strong military states.

Inasmuch as Italy has signed no minorities treaties and so

is under no international obligations to protect the rights of her minorities, she has done just about as she pleased with them. And it has pleased Italy to try to turn them into good Italians in a few years. She has kept Slavs and Germans out of official positions—even out of such jobs as the management of cooperatives—in the regions where the Slav and German minorities live. She has banned their newspapers and their languages and made them conduct all their business and post all their public notices in Italian. Slav and German children may not even sing Slav and German songs, or be called by Slav or German names.

Naturally the voices of Germans, Croats and Slovenes have been raised in bitter complaint against the Italianization policies of the Italian government. Italians report that their national safety depends upon the success of their campaign to stamp out the national consciousness of their minorities. But the experience of history spells failure for this attempt to make Slavs and Germans into Italians.

ITALY AND YUGOSLAVIA

For nearly twenty years after the World War the Italians and Yugoslavs were at swords' points. Under these conditions each national minority in the country of the other suffered from the feud between Italy and Yugoslavia. In 1937, Mussolini, deeply involved in Ethiopia and Spain, needed to protect his rear from a possible war with the South Slavs. So, as we have seen, the tension between the two countries eased. But the change did not solve the problems outstanding between them.

ITALY AND AUSTRIA

As we have pointed out, the boundary drawn by the Peace Conference between Italy and Austria was a strategic frontier. It was in no sense drawn in accordance with the principle of self-determination. Italy, one of the winners in the war, was determined to hold the enormously important Brenner Pass, although she could not hold the Brenner without including a German minority within her borders. This minority lives in the district known as South Tyrol.

For many years Italy tried to turn these former Austrians into Italians. She forbade them to have their own German schools; suppressed their German-language newspapers; even obliged them to change their German names to Italian. But all in vain: the Austrians of South Tyrol remained stubbornly Austrian.

Finally, in July 1939 Hitler and Mussolini reached an agreement by which these former Austrians, numbering more than 200,000, were to choose between moving to the Reich and becoming good Italian Fascisti. Details of the agreement were not yet known when this book went to press. But it seemed sure to impose further hardships on the already sorely tried Tyroleans. The purpose of the move was apparently to destroy any claim Germany might have to South Tyrol, and so eliminate a possible cause of friction between the two partners in the so-called "Rome-Berlin axis."

DENMARK'S MINORITY

Striking north from Italy, across Great Germany, we come to the border of the kingdom of Denmark (center map). Here everything looks peaceful. Here, it would seem, there is good will between men. There are few soldiers to be seen. In fact, the boundary seems quite unlike so many of the warlike frontiers that we have crossed during our journey about Europe.

But appearances are deceptive. For this frontier between the Third Reich and Denmark is one of the "bleeding borders" that the Nazis denounce. In May 1938, it is true, the Reich and Denmark signed a non-aggression pact. Nevertheless the question of border revision still remains.

But is it, in reality, a border that was drawn in defiance of German rights? Perhaps we ought to look briefly into that question.

DENMARK AT THE PEACE CONFERENCE

When the Peace Conference assembled in Paris early in 1919, it was generally believed that Denmark could expect sympathetic consideration of any territorial claims she might make against defeated Germany. Had not the Prussians and Austrians attacked little Denmark in 1864? Had those powers not torn away a large slice of Danish territory? And was not the northern part of the German province of Schleswig inhabited by a Danish majority?

Yes, Denmark had these territorial claims against the Reich. Had the Danes chosen to do so, they might have made a successful claim for a large tract of German territory at the Conference. They might have turned the tables on their large neighbor by taking districts in which there was a German majority and only a small Danish minority.

But the Danes were too far-sighted to make extravagant claims against the defeated Germans. Unlike certain other countries, Denmark refused to take advantage of Allied victory. The Danes asked merely for a rectification of the Danish-German frontier that would carry out the ideal of "self-determination." They would accept only territory in which there was an unquestioned Danish majority.

"BLEEDING BORDER"?

The result of this Danish policy was that, when the frontier between Denmark and Germany was finally drawn, it was as nearly perfect as any frontier could be that divided a region of mixed nationality groups. Plebiscites conducted honestly and efficiently helped make possible the establishment of a reasonable border, leaving only a few thousand Danes in Germany and a few thousand Germans in Denmark. If anything, there are now more Danes in Germany than Germans in Denmark. Consequently Nazi charges that this is a "bleeding border" look pretty much like nonsense.

THE GERMANS IN DENMARK

Furthermore, the Danish constitution contains adequate safeguards for a minority people. For that reason the Peace Conference imposed no special obligations on Denmark in regard to the German minority. Indeed, the Danish government gives the German minority every opportunity to develop its own culture. German children in South Jutland (North Schleswig to the Nazis) may go to Danish or German schools, as their parents choose. And the German private schools receive state grants for their support. It is hardly necessary to add that the Danish minority in Germany receives no such privileges from the Nazis.

During the days of the German Republic there was no serious territorial dispute between Germany and Denmark. The democratic régime in Berlin recognized the enlightened and friendly attitude displayed by the Danes toward Germany. The "bleeding border" propaganda did not loom large until the Nazis became active. And it did not become a grave international issue until Hitler and his followers took over the German government in January 1933. We shall return to this subject a little later, when we discuss the Third Reich and its policies toward the German minorities.

SWITZERLAND

We have visited country after country where minority problems threaten internal peace and the orderly course of international relations. After such a journey it may be a relief to survey the situation in a country where there is no strife among the various peoples who compose the population. Such a state is Switzerland.

This mountain republic in the heart of Europe is inhabited mainly by German-, French- and Italian-speaking peoples. The German part of the population is the most numerous, representing a little over seventy per cent of the inhabitants. The French-speaking citizens number about twenty per cent and the Italian-speaking people about six per cent. Moreover, each of the three major language groups lives in territory bordering on a great power whose language and cultural relationship is very close. But in spite of this fact the people of Switzerland do not consider themselves Germans, or Frenchmen, or Italians. They are Swiss.

And so in Switzerland there are no national minorities. The various language groups of the republic get along well together and there is no irreconcilable minority clamoring for reunion with its brothers across some frontier.

But this happy state of affairs is not due to good neighborliness toward the Swiss on the part of some of the great powers which surround the little republic. On the contrary, there have been, and still are, strenuous efforts made by certain powers (mainly Germany, but to some extent also Italy) to influence the Swiss to think and act in terms of so-called "racial origin."

Nevertheless, the German-, French- and Italian-speaking Swiss all persevere in being unqualifiedly Swiss. Their loyalty is to their own progressive and pacific little state. Their common sense and tolerance are effective defenses against the ideological struggles, racial persecution and minority strife that plague the countries bordering on Switzerland. Yes, democratic Switzerland is a haven of peace and enlightenment in an age when civilization is on the defensive in many parts of the world. It is the ideal toward which all the minorities disputants might well aim.

VII. Efforts to Solve Minority Problems

In the early post-war era there were several attempts to alleviate, if not to solve, specific minority problems in certain areas of Europe. One way of dealing with the problem was to transfer minority populations from the state where they were living to the state where they belonged, or thought they belonged. Another was the League's way of handling them. In this chapter we shall briefly describe both of these methods.

THE TURKS EXPEL THEIR GREEK MINORITY

The most ambitious attempt to transfer minority peoples was made by Turkey and Greece. As we have seen, in 1922 the Turks drove more than a million Greeks out of Turkey. There were Armenians, too, in this exodus. These wretched people, the majority of whom were women, old men and children, sought refuge on the islands and mainland of Greece. Some of them, however, could not speak Greek. The only language they knew was Turkish. To add to their misery, Greece was suffering from the economic strain of several years of war.

We may get some idea of the seriousness of the refugee problem in Greece at that time when we realize that the population of that country was suddenly increased by approximately twenty-five per cent. Suppose, for instance, that we in America were suddenly confronted with the enormous problem of caring for more than *thirty million* refugees! To make matters worse, suppose these refugees brought with them little except the clothes on their backs. Suppose many of them were sick and some had serious diseases like typhus, typhoid, smallpox and trachoma. How could we cope with such a situation thrust upon us without warning?

GREECE CALLS FOR HELP

Well, the Greek government and people found the problem too big for their resources. They called for help from abroad. And without delay America answered their cry of distress. The American Red Cross and the Near East Relief bore the brunt of the relief work. While schools, theaters, empty buildings of all kinds and even old railway cars and abandoned ships were used as shelters, the refugees went to work to build temporary housing. In time hamlets grew up, peopled entirely by the exiles.

In spite of the fact that most of their young men had either been killed by the Turks or kept behind as prisoners, the refugees displayed a strong morale. They were down but by no means out. As the months passed the newcomers gradually began to find work; many of them started small home industries. Before long there were marriages between refugees and natives. The refugee children quickly learned the Greek language, adopted Greek customs and began to be assimilated by the various communities in which they found themselves.

In spite of this exodus of Greeks from Turkey, thousands of Greeks still remained in Turkish territory. And there were thousands of Turks in Greece, located principally in Greek Macedonia and on the island of Crete.

A PLAN OF ACTION EMERGES

In 1923 a change in Turko-Greek relations began to develop. It was slow, to be sure, but it followed the right direction. At first it was a desire by both governments to do something to relieve the sufferings of the refugees on both sides of the Turko-Greek frontier. There were conversations between Turks and Greeks through neutral third parties and eventually direct contacts between the Turkish and Greek governments.

From these experimental talks, a plan of action began to assume form. It was constructively furthered by the Near East

Relief. Finally, both parties agreed that an exchange of minorities should be carried out. It was to be a compulsory exchange.

GREECE AND TURKEY EXCHANGE MINORITIES

The plan of exchange, it is true, did make certain exceptions. The Greeks in Istambul and the Turks in Western Thrace were not compelled to emigrate. But Turks in other parts of Greece and Greeks in other parts of Turkey were forced to pack up their portable goods and move.

We state that fact in a few words. Yet it would take literally thousands of words to tell, in terms of human suffering, even a very incomplete story of this exchange of minorities. And unless you have seen a population of refugees in flight you can scarcely conceive what such a migration means in terms of human misery and cruelty. But anyone who *has* seen such a sight is sure to be slow to suggest an exchange of populations as the solution of the minorities problem. In the case of the Greeks and Turks, of course, it must be kept in mind that the early part of the exchange was chaotic: it was carried out under war conditions. But the later and orderly part of it was conducted under the most favorable circumstances. Yet even the help of neutrals and the cooperation of Greeks and Turks could not prevent losses, grief and suffering to thousands of people. This drastic exchange did, however, put an end to the centuries-old Turko-Greek feud.

OTHER MINORITY MIGRATIONS

As a rule, governments which hope for territorial revision believe that an exchange of minority populations removes the justification for such a change of frontiers as they desire. So they hesitate to exchange their minority populations.

Nevertheless, early in the post-war era Greece and Bulgaria made an attempt to solve their mutual minorities problems by a reciprocal exchange of population. The exchange did not proceed with any marked success, however, because the Bulgars in Greece and the Greeks in Bulgaria objected to leaving their ancestral homes and moving to a strange community.

After the war, too, Greece and Rumania arranged for some of the Vlachs (Rumanians) of Greece to return to the Rumanian motherland. And a small, voluntary and unsupervised movement of Serbs from Albania to Yugoslavia took place about seven years ago.

A few years ago, the Rumanian and Turkish governments tried out still another experiment in transplanting minorities. Thanks to the fact that the two governments were on friendly terms, the arrangement was made under the most favorable conditions. In brief, it was an attempt to move the Turkish minority in Rumanian Dobrudja to Anatolia, a district of Turkey (center map).

Finally, as we have already seen, Italy and Germany have recently agreed on a forced migration of the former Austrians living in the Italian Tyrol.

These smaller migrations have been mentioned to round out our story. But they are not put forth as solutions of the minority problem. For only an irresponsible person would suggest that a wholesale migration of thirty or forty million people should be started. A drastic experiment of this kind would result in chaos and suffering such as Europe has not seen since the Thirty Years' War (1618-1648). Certainly so ill-advised a venture would create far more problems than it solved.

THE LEAGUE AND MINORITIES

In the decade that followed the Turko-Greek exchange of minorities, the only other attempts that were made to improve the lot of minorities were those of the League of Nations. But the League was hampered by lack of sufficient power to deal adequately with the problem.

As we saw in Chapter III, clauses governing the treatment of minorities were written into some of the peace treaties. At the same time, Czechoslovakia, Greece, Poland, Rumania and Yugoslavia signed special treaties with the Allied Powers known as the Minorities Treaties. Later Albania and the Baltic states entered into similar agreements before the League.

All of these agreements guaranteed to minority peoples in the first place a number of general rights: the right to citizenship, personal liberty and freedom of worship; equality with the other citizens of the state before the law; freedom from discrimination in public employment and in the exercise of professions and industries; the right to use their own language; and the right to establish their own schools and charitable institutions, with aid from whatever public funds were available. In the second place, the agreements admitted that it was the concern of the League to see that they were enforced.

The idea behind these agreements was certainly an advance. It meant that all the signatories agreed to submit their minority disputes to an international body, instead of trying to dispose of them through political bargaining among the powers, as they had done before. But the new system of guarantees for minorities did not include all European countries and it lacked any real method of enforcement. For the League can act in a matter concerning a minority only *if a member of the Council of the League brings to the Council's attention a violation or danger of violation of the minorities provisions.*

Nevertheless, in spite of having its hands tied most of the time where the minorities are concerned, the League has done some good work in the field. A special section of the League Secretariat has collected a mass of information to aid the Council in its discussion on minorities problems. In practice the Council (or its committees) has played the role of conciliator between governments and their minorities (or other governments interested in their minorities). Nearly 900 petitions have been addressed to the League and more than half of them have been accepted and acted upon.

It was little enough, however, that the League could do, measured by the size of the whole problem.

THE MINORITIES BECOME SCAPEGOATS

In all too many cases the minorities were used as scapegoats. When a government made a mistake, the minorities could be blamed. When new land or money was needed, the minorities could be dispossessed. When the minorities protested, their spokesmen were in many cases arrested and imprisoned. And when a minority was maltreated, its brethren across the frontier were almost certain to protest vigorously.

This state of affairs not only prevented a normal way of life in the affected areas. It undermined the efforts of a few sincere men, like the late Aristide Briand of France, who were endeavoring to lay the foundations for an enduring peace. But Europe's minorities problem assumed its most acute form only after the Nazis came to power in Germany.

VIII. The Nazis and the German Minorities

We have mentioned earlier in the book that the Nazis hold extreme theories about "race" and nationality. As we have pointed out, these theories are refuted by science, history and human experience. Yet they are spread by men who control one of the greatest military machines in the world. For that reason we must examine these views. We must study them and interpret them in terms of what is happening to minorities over a large part of Europe today.

First, we must realize that Hitler and his followers propagate the myth of a "superior race." They teach their young people that the German stands above all other men, that the German is a "superman." If the Nazis merely repeated this tale to bolster up their self-confidence, we might pass it by as of little consequence. It so happens, however, that the Nazis' theory of German "racial superiority" is the basis of their foreign policy. It is the foundation of their treatment of the minorities within the Reich. It is the driving power of their propaganda. And, as we shall see, it is the rallying cry of their new Brown-Shirt imperialism.

THE JEWS AND THE MINORITY PROBLEM

We have used the words "ancestry, traditions, language, culture or religion" in our definition of a minority. Now a group might be a minority in one country and not in another. As an illustration of this point take the Jews. The Jews are not a minority in the Scandinavian countries and the Western democracies. A Jew who is a citizen of Sweden, for instance, is simply a Swedish citizen of the Jewish faith. The same thing is true of the Jews in the other Norse countries, as well as in Holland, Belgium, Switzerland, France, Britain and the Dominions, in Ireland, and in the United States. Until recently it was the case in Italy. Even as late as January 1933, it was true in Germany.

But it was not the case in Tsarist Russia. In that vast empire the Jews were persecuted as an alien people. They were not allowed to move about the country freely, practice certain professions or engage in certain educational and economic pursuits. Before the World War, emigration afforded the Jews in Russia some relief. But those who remained in the Tsar's territory were compelled to suffer terrible persecution.

It has been said that in pre-Hitler Germany many Jews were "more German than the Germans." Not a few were members of the Nationalist Party. In the World War Jewish scientists discovered invaluable ways to make up for the Reich's lack of certain essential raw materails. Thousands of other German Jews gave their lives on the battlefields of the World War fighting for their country—the Reich. Many of them were decorated for bravery. But no matter. The Nazis set out to exterminate the Jews who live in Germany. They even erased the names of the Jewish war dead from the monuments.

It is ironical to recall that at Versailles the Germans were not required to give ironclad guarantees that they would treat their minorities justly. But the truth is that they were not. For it was assumed that, as a highly civilized state, Germany would not do otherwise than treat her minorities justly. And that assumption was certainly true of the Germany of 1919; indeed, it was true of the Germany of 1932. But it has not been true of the Third Reich of Adolf Hitler and his Nazis. For the National Socialists recognize no obligation to treat their minorities as if they were human beings. Germany is "master of her own house!" the Nazis boast. And those whom they consider non-Germans must suffer accordingly. Of all those who have been persecuted in Germany, the Jews have been singled out for the most extreme kind of oppression.

THE JEWS IN EAST-CENTRAL EUROPE

But discrimination against the Jews does not stop with Germany and Italy, the two principal Fascist countries. It extends throughout most of East-Central Europe, where more than five million Jews live. There is now scarcely a nation in that entire area which does not exert some kind of pressure against the Jewish part of its population. Some of this persecution can be ascribed to bad economic conditions; some of it is due to religious bigotry, some of it to political fanaticism, and some of it to age-old prejudice.

Above all, the Jews are often the scapegoats. When economic conditions are bad, blame can be conveniently laid on them. When governments fail to carry out their promises, they can blame their own shortcomings on the Jews.

We must keep in mind the fact that the Minorities Treaties were meant to protect the Jews as well as the other minorities of East-Central Europe. A large majority of the representatives of the Jews of East-Central Europe viewed their people as a minority and desired to be called a minority in the Minorities Treaties. Of course, this fact did not in any way affect the loyalty of the Jews to the governments under which they lived. Under these treaties the Jews and all other minorities could speak their own languages and cherish their own peculiar cultural traditions. As badly as these Minorities Treaties have been abused, there can be little doubt that they have helped the situation. Nevertheless the plight of the Jews in Germany and East-Central Europe has been a deplorable blot on our twentieth century civilization.

THE NAZIS AND PAN-GERMANISM

Like the men who ruled the Reich in the years before the World War, Hitler and his Nazis are striving to build a great empire. They, too, have dreamed of uniting the nearly one hundred million Germans in Europe into one great military state. Right now those dreams are being translated into action. Already we have seen the Third Reich annex Austria, seize Memel, incorporate within Great Germany nearly all of Czechoslovakia and, finally, attack and invade Poland.

It would be wrong, however, to convey the idea that Nazi Germany is just the old monarchy dressed in a brown shirt. The Germany of today is a very different state from the pre-war Reich. In those days there was in Germany a measure of liberalism and a measure of democracy. Today, the Third Reich is a totalitarian dictatorship. Yet to further its ends, it carries on the program of the Pan-Germans. The methods are changed; but the general direction is the same.

Now, as we learned early in the book, there are German minorities scattered across Europe from the Gulf of Finland to the Danube-Save line in Yugoslavia, and from Alsace-Lorraine in the West almost to the Urals in the East (map, p. 27). Some of these German groups have lived in their present homes for centuries. Some of them went into these distant regions in search of better farming lands. Others—the Saxons in Rumania, for example—left the land that is now Germany to serve in foreign armies. Catherine of Russia invited German colonists to her vast country because she needed good farmers.

But when a German group left the region of its ancestors and traveled hundreds of miles to a new home, its members did not shed their Germanism. They did not become Russians, or Rumanians, or Magyars. They remained Germans. They kept their German language, their German customs, their German outlook. Furthermore, many of the Germans who lived in the countries of Eastern and Central Europe before the World War were more prosperous than their Slavic, Latin or Magyar neighbors.

THE GERMAN MINORITIES AFTER THE WAR

The peace treaties directly affected the status of the German minorities. No longer could the German in one of the new states maintain his old supremacy. For he soon found that the once despised native—whether that native was an Esth, a Rumanian or a Czech—now held the upper hand. He found that his old influence with the imperial government was as dead as that government itself. Furthermore, he learned that when he tried to carry on his trade he was forced to operate under new rules, rules that were written by the new masters. And he soon discovered that the many newly drawn frontiers interfered with his commerce: there were new tariff barriers.

The German outside Germany blamed most of these difficulties on the government under which he was now living. And it is only fair to concede that all too often some of the new governments were not generous—or even far-sighted—in their policies toward the German minorities. The former under dog was now top dog. And his resentment against the recent economic supremacy of the Germans now took the form of oppressive measures directed against his German neighbors.

OPPRESSION BEGETS OPPRESSION

Perhaps it would have been too much to expect the new majority governments to adopt a more tolerant attitude toward their minorities than the treatment they themselves had received as minorities. Yet, even though we may understand this maltreatment of the German minorities after the war, we cannot condone it on either ethical or political grounds. And the worst of it is that wherever there has been discrimination against a Germanic minority anywhere in Europe, that discrimination has played directly into the hands of the Nazis.

THE GRIEVANCES OF THE GERMAN MINORITIES

Whenever the Nazi agents found a dissatisfied German group anywhere they were quick to capitalize the grievances of these people. When there was no real grievance, as in the case of the German minority in Denmark, the Nazis proceeded to manufacture one.

But the point to keep in mind is this: nearly everywhere the German minorities had some cause for complaint. And the Nazi agents lost no time in uncovering all real causes of discontent among the German minorities and quickly proceeded to exaggerate them.

In the next chapter we shall see just how the Nazis went about their work with the Germans abroad.

IX. Nazi Methods

If we had been in Latvia, or any of several other countries a few months ago, we might have seen people entering a house by twos and threes. If we had asked some one about them we should have learned that they were Germans, legally citizens of the country in which they lived, but spiritually part of the Pan-German realm. They had all been influenced by National Socialism. They were as ardently pro-Nazi as any similar group of men and women inside Germany.

NAZI PROPAGANDA ON THE AIR

They were going to a meeting in the house of their local Fuehrer. If we had entered the house we should have found these people sitting around a radio listening to a speech broadcast to them from the Reich. If it had been early September, we might have heard Hitler's voice screaming at them from the colossal annual Nazi Party Congress at Nuremberg. Or if it had been Christmas time, we might have heard the voice of Rudolph Hess, deputy Nazy Party leader, telling them that Chancellor Hitler had given Germans, in place of the Bolshevist ideal of destruction, a genuinely religious ideal of reconstruction.

If we had been listening to Marshal Goering, the Number Two Nazi, on September 2, 1937, we should have heard him shout these words to all the German minorities: "The Nazi government expects every German residing abroad to put the interests of the Fatherland before his own."

Pounding home his message, Marshal Goering explained: "You foreign Germans must remember that wherever you are, you represent the interests of Germany. The Fatherland must come first. All else is second!"

These speeches from the Reich to the German minorities all over the world were supplemented by musical programs, weather forecasts, crop reports, cooking hints, dramatic sketches and "news reports." We may be certain that the Propaganda Ministry prepared the "news reports" carefully. Nothing, we may be sure, crept into them that was not highly favorable to the Nazis. But whatever the program might be, it was part of the radio propaganda drive to bind the German minorities to the homeland.

PROPAGANDA IN THE MOVIES

In addition to the Nazi radio propaganda, there was propaganda by moving pictures. In America we have a system of motion picture censorship. It is concerned almost entirely with moral questions. In Germany, too, there was a censorship, but it dealt primarily with political questions. It was inconceivable that any film could be made in Nazi Germany which conflicted with Nazi ideas. But if such a miracle took place, we may be sure that the German people never saw the picture.

Now let's see what happened when one of these films was completed. It was, of course, shown in the movie houses throughout the Reich. After the film had been shown in Germany it was sent abroad. In many of these films the "superiority" of the German people was emphasized and the power of the Third Reich was driven home to all who saw the pictures. Since, in country after country of East-Central Europe, the members of the German minorities went to see the German-made films, this call to the German minorities was likely to have its effect.

Furthermore, in countries like Latvia and Estonia, where nearly everybody, at least in the cities, understands a little German, the German sound films influenced the non-German part of the population too. Unconsciously, perhaps, those who saw the pictures were influenced to think in terms of German prestige, German armed might, German commercial and industrial leadership.

HOW NAZI PROPAGANDA FILMS WORKED

Now there is a subtle side of this situation that the American reader might not suspect. For the average American doesn't think like a member of a European minority. In Europe, except in rare instances, the members of a minority group feel some sense of insecurity, some feeling of resentment against the treatment they receive from the majority. More often than not the majority population, unwittingly perhaps, inspires in the minority a sense of inferiority. This psychological factor is an important part of the entire minority problem. It is not confined to any one people.

Take, for instance, the German who lived in Hungary. When the German propaganda film was shown in his community, he was delighted. It might impress his non-German neighbors with the power and excellence of the Third Reich. Consequently, he may have believed, it would make these neighbors a little more careful in their relations with him. For didn't they see on the screen pictures that showed the prowess and glories of the German nation—*his* Fatherland?

NAZI PROPAGANDA AND THE PRESS

Still another propaganda tool is the press. We know, of course, that the entire press of Germany has been "coordinated." No independent newspaper can exist anywhere in that totalitarian state. But it is not so well understood in America that the German press is by no means confined within the borders of the Reich. There are German-language newspapers in many of the countries of Europe. Naturally, most of these journals present the German point of view. But not all of them present the Nazi point of view. For the Nazi point of view and the German point of view are by no means the same thing.

Take the German-language newspaper of a town in pre-Munich Czechoslovakia. This journal may have been intensely loyal to the German way of thought. But it was directly opposed to the Nazi *Weltanschauung* (world outlook). It may have been Social Democratic, it may have been Catholic, or it may not have had any political or religious affiliation at all. It may have been merely liberal in its viewpoint. If this was the case, it repudiated Nazi propaganda. It went even further, in all probability, and defended its democratic ideals against Nazism.

HOW GOEBBELS DEALS WITH A FREE PRESS

When Dr. Goebbels encountered such an independent German-language newspaper anywhere in Europe he could proceed against it by any one of several methods. He could try to buy it. If that failed, he could attempt to stir up the local German population against its editors. He could organize a boycott. If this, too, failed, he might bring pressure against the government of the country to censor the pages of the offending paper. In fact, he might even demand that it be suppressed. As a rule, one of these methods was effective. The newspaper in question either conformed to Nazi policies or was put out of business.

THE NAZIS BRIBE THE FOREIGN PRESS

We have been discussing the newspapers of the German minorities. Now let's turn for a moment to newspapers published in other languages, the native-tongue journals in countries outside Germany. Were these newspapers all independent and honestly edited? No, indeed. Some of them lived by means of subsidies from abroad. In other words, they took bribes for publishing propaganda. This is not new. In fact, it is an old, old custom in Europe and elsewhere.

Even though the bribery of European newspapers is an old custom the Nazis added some new wrinkles to it. They conducted it on a larger and more thorough scale than ever before. They perfected the technique of journalistic bribery.

REICH PROPAGANDA ORGANIZATIONS

The Nazi campaign to convert all Germans living abroad into good National Socialists was by no means confined to the radio, the cinema and the press. Coordinated with this Nazi propaganda was the work of various special Nazi organizations which dealt entirely with Germans in foreign countries.

In late August 1937, the Foreign Organization of the Nazi Party held an annual conference at Stuttgart, in southern Germany. At the conference Herr Ernst Bohle, British-born leader of the Foreign Organization, declared that by decree the Fuehrer had made "the Foreign Organization of the Nazi Party, a branch of the German Foreign Ministry." This decree gave Herr Bohle's representatives in foreign lands diplomatic status, and brought all German citizens living or traveling abroad under his direct jurisdiction. They were not asked, but commanded, to be good Nazis and to greet one another with "Heil Hitler!"

With Germans who are not citizens of the Reich but of the countries in which they are living, the Nazis could not openly take so imperious a tone. But, up to the outbreak of war, at least, there was a bureau in Berlin which existed solely to "cooperate" with the organizations of Germans of foreign citizenship in cultural matters. It kept in close touch with the German minorities, sent books, magazines and newspapers to the scattered German colonies and dispatched political missionaries and teachers to the spots that needed Nazi cultivation.

WHISPER PROPAGANDA

One of the most effective methods Nazi agents used to line up the German minorities for Hitler was "whisper propaganda." All kinds of exaggerated stories were spread by word of mouth to frighten non-Nazis. "Hitler is coming! Heads will roll!" was whispered throughout Austria before the Nazis marched in. It was used effectively in Memel and Czechoslovakia. It was being used in Denmark, the Baltic states, Hungary, Rumania, Yugoslavia and other countries a few months ago.

BOYCOTT AND SOCIAL OSTRACISM

But the Nazis found even more powerful methods of bringing their minorities into line. As we have observed, not all members of the German minorities were sympathetic to Hitlerism. For various reasons they found the Nazi ideology abhorrent. They preferred to remain at peace with their neighbors and to be loyal citizens of the respective nations in which they lived.

But the Nazis had ruthless, and usually effective, ways of dealing with these recalcitrant members of the German groups. The boycott, for instance, was used very effectively. We find, say, that a German merchant living in Hungary is a Social Democrat. He bears no enmity toward even the Third Reich of Adolf Hitler. But he wants to be let alone. When he is visited by Nazi agents, he declines to bow to their threats.

Very well, then, the local agents of Hitler know how to deal with him. His store suddenly loses all its business with the National Socialist element in the community. But that isn't all. The Nazis have still other means of hounding him. It is not enough to forbid the Hitlerites to purchase goods at his store. All other Germans in the region must also boycott it. If they hesitate, the same tactics are used against them.

Thus before long the Social Democrat was likely to find that his business was ruined. He could do only one of two things: he could join the Nazis, or he could leave the community. If he chose the latter alternative, he was likely soon to encounter the same coercion from other Nazis at his next stop.

ANTI-SEMITISM AND THE GERMAN GROUPS

Another outstanding feature of the Nazi propaganda among the German minorities was anti-Semitism. Hitler, Goebbels, Streicher and Rosenberg used every resource at their command to sow hatred of the Jew among the Germanic groups everywhere.

For middle-class Germans the Jew was pictured as a Bolshevik. The agents of Hitler spread the tale that the Jew was plotting against Western civilization, against the home, the Church and, above all, the German Fatherland. The Jew was portrayed as the agent of Stalin. It was the Jew, said the Nazi agents, who spread war, pestilence and destruction.

To influence the poor member of the German minority, the Nazis pictured the Jew as the international capitalist. It was the Jew, so the poor of the minorities were told, who kept down the prices of the commodities the poor produce. When the poor had to buy anything, it was the Jew again. He kept the price high. When the poor German had to borrow money, it was the Jew once more. The extortioner might be a rich member of the German minority. But no matter. The Jew was blamed as the invisible extortioner who kept interest charges high.

And so we find that among the German minorities in particular, and among the other nationalities in general, the propaganda from Berlin had a sharp anti-Semitic bias.

"BLOOD KNOWS NO NATIONAL FRONTIERS!"

So much for the organizations of Nazi propaganda among the German minority groups. What was the underlying purpose of all this activity?

The underlying purpose was to create a great German empire in Europe—and even beyond Europe. When the Nazis shout: "Blood knows no national frontiers!" they mean exactly what they say. They voice their contention that wherever German minorities live, there also is Germany. In plain words, the Nazis mean that there is land in Lithuania, Poland, Denmark, France, Switzerland, Yugoslavia, Hungary, Rumania, Estonia, the Soviet Union and Latvia that belongs to them. This is the land which is inhabited by German minorities.

The Nazi watchword, *Volksgemeinschaft* [blood brotherhood], means the unification of all the Germans under one flag. Or, as the Nazis put it, "One people, one Reich, one leader."

Naturally, the political activities of the German minorities brought counter-action from the governments under which they lived. In many cases the discrimination against the Germanic groups increased. This was partly due to the Nazi interference. In certain cases, however, pressure from the German government compelled a small nation to grant greater "cultural rights" to its German minority. This really meant greater freedom to make trouble.

But in most cases the German minorities listened to the Nazis because the members of these German minorities resented the treatment they had received at the hands of the majority and believed it was unjust. So when the majority people discovered the Nazi activities in their country and, in consequence, bore down still harder on the German minority, a vicious circle was created. Thus whether they gave in to the demands of their German minorities or resisted them all the more resolutely, the governments of East-Central Europe were faced with a dilemma.

TRADE PRESSURE

It was not merely with propaganda that the German minorities were pursued. In the Third Reich of Adolf Hitler politics and economics walk hand in hand. And in foreign relations, diplomacy and trade are inextricably intertwined. Denmark is a good example of this trade pressure. Before the present war, Germany was Denmark's second best customer. The Danes didn't like this situation, but they didn't seem to be able to escape from it. Now suppose that the Danish government had taken determined action to curb the growing Nazi influence over the German minority in Denmark. This would probably have brought drastic reprisals from the Reich. Hitler could have suddenly stopped all German imports of Danish butter, cattle, hogs and eggs. That would have been a terrific blow to Danish economy. It would have inflicted severe hardships on the Danes. But that was what would probably have happened if, for political reasons, Hitler had decided to "teach the Danes a lesson."

X. Hitler's Human Dynamite

We have already seen how Hitler has used the Germans living outside the borders of the Third Reich as an excuse to enlarge his realm: how in March 1938 he sent his army into Austria in order, as he said, to save the Austrian Germans from the "bludgeons" of their "tormentors"; how in September 1938 he obtained the Sudeten areas of Czechoslovakia because they were inhabited by Germans who, he claimed, were being persecuted by the Czechs; how in March 1939 he took most of the rest of Czechoslovakia and Memel on much the same sort of pretext; and how in September 1939 he invaded Poland.

Unfortunately, now that a general war has broken out, and Great Britain and France are fighting not only to defend Poland but also to get rid of Hitlerism, the situation has changed radically, and it is too soon to know for certain what use a Germany at war will make of the German minorities in other countries. But at least we can see what use she was making of them just before the war began, and perhaps from this we can get some inkling of what will happen now.

THE SITUATION IN DENMARK

The chart on page 83 shows the number of Germans living in each of the principal countries of Europe today. Suppose we begin our survey with Denmark. By the beginning of 1939 the Danish government and people were becoming increasingly uneasy about the Nazi penetration of the little kingdom of Hans Christian Andersen. It is true that the Nazis there had been guilty of little actual violence. Their activities had been confined largely to propaganda and organization. In Copenhagen there was a Nazi newspaper, the *National Socialisten*, with the swastika ("the cross that is not the cross of Christ") on its front page. Young men in the uniforms of Nazi Storm Troopers could be seen on the streets of the Danish capital. Their noise however, was more impressive than their numbers. But their presence was a portent of trouble.

In the Danish province of South Jutland, or North Schleswig, as the Germans call it (center map), National Socialist propaganda proceeded steadily. Pressure was exerted against those members of the German minority who did not cooperate with the campaign to wrest this region away from Denmark. The same harsh methods to drive the recalcitrants into line were used here as elsewhere. And the Danish authorities were seriously concerned about the German government's practice of advancing loans to Germans in Denmark to increase the land holdings of the German minority.

IN LITHUANIA

The Nazis made striking progress in Lithuania also. The Memel territory, with its Lithuanian minority, went back to the Reich. This cession entailed great losses and hardships for the non-Nazi German part of the Memelland population. Although there were only a few thousand Germans left in the rest of Lithuania, many informed observers expected the Nazis to use them as a pretext to make more trouble for the Lithuanian government some time in the future.

IN LATVIA

Across Lithuania's northern border the Letts too were confronted with the economic and political offensive of Nazi Ger-

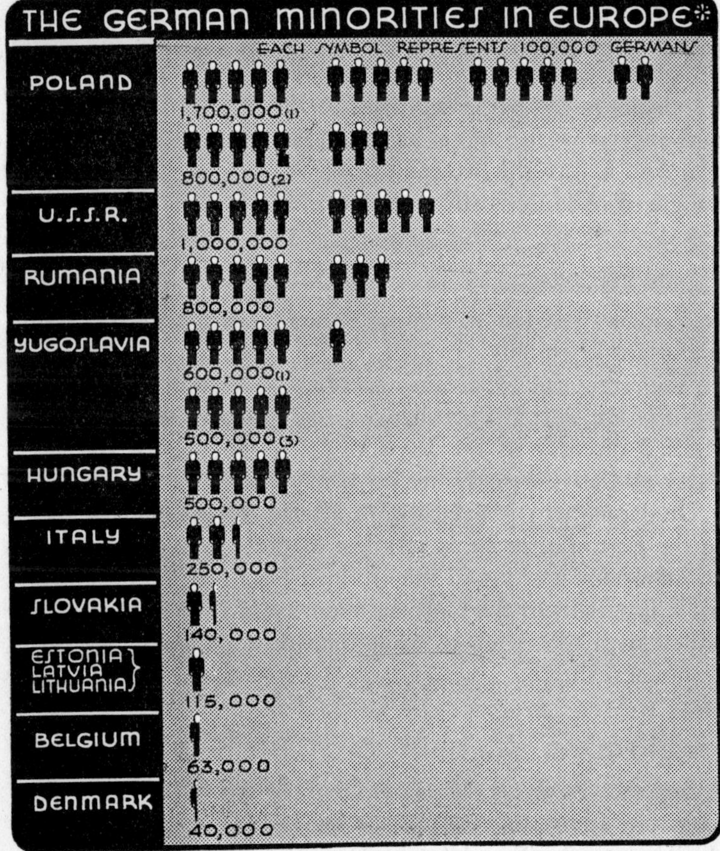

* All figures are approximate, being based on the best available estimates.

[1] German estimate.

[2] Polish estimate.

[3] Yugoslav estimate.

many. For Latvia, like Lithuania and Estonia, is located on the northeast route of the *Drang nach Osten* [drive to the East] (map, p. 31).

The German minority in Latvia consists of about 70,000 people. It is small, in comparison with the German minorities in several other states, but it is important. These German minorities in the Baltic states are the descendants of the proud and once powerful Baltic barons. They are a determined people. And before the present war began, at least, they were the vanguard of Hitler's advance toward the Gulf of Finland.

IN ESTONIA

In Estonia there are only about 18,000 Germans. They are not important in numbers, perhaps, but in other respects they play an important role. The Estonian capital, Tallinn, is the home town of Dr. Alfred Rosenberg, "prophet laureate of the Third Reich," director of the Foreign Affairs Section of the Nazi Party and adviser to Hitler on foreign policies.

Dr. Rosenberg is a fanatical advocate of the revived drive to the East. Today he is a citizen of the Reich and maintains an important position in the German Nazi régime. In the past his fellow Balts of the German minority in Estonia have cooperated with the Reich to make the dream of a great German empire a reality.

IN POLAND

Along the German-Polish frontier there are mixed nationality areas too (map, p. 35). On the map the German and Polish shadings run back and forth across the common border, but they seldom blend. The Germans intended to regain the territory they lost to Poland. The Poles knew of Germany's intention and were resolved to retain every square mile of their country. Consequently for several months there was little more than an armed truce between these two neighbors, and even before the beginning of hostilities life was difficult for both the Germans in Poland and the Poles in Germany.

In order to defend the Corridor (center map) the Poles began quietly moving the German minority out of the disputed region. They had good grounds for their suspicions that Hitler was using the German minority in Poland to further Nazi plans.

DANZIG

The chief bone of contention between Poland and Germany, however, was the Free City of Danzig. Before the war, Danzig was a part of the Reich. But when Poland was restored as an independent state by the Paris Peace Conference, Danzig presented a problem. Its population was almost wholly German: therefore it could not be handed over to Poland without violating the principle of self-determination. On the other hand, without it Poland would have no seaport.

This problem the Peace Conference solved by setting up Danzig as a "free city"—a tiny independent state—under the protection of the League. Thus after 1919 Danzig had its own parliament and its own police force. But in order to see that the rights of Germany, Poland and the native population were respected, it also had a League of Nations commissioner responsible only to the League at Geneva.

Now Germany protested against this arrangement ever since it was made. And Poland prepared for the day when Danzig might return to the Reich by building a seaport of her own on the site of what was once the tiny fishing village of Gdynia, in the "Corridor."

HITLER'S DEMANDS

In August 1939 Hitler demanded the immediate return of the Free City, and threatened to go to war if his demand were not heeded. But Poland refused to permit Danzig to be returned, for she believed that Germany would use it as the spearhead of a drive to cut off the Corridor. In fact, Germany had already made her ultimate intentions clear by demanding the cession of a strip of territory across the Polish Corridor to connect East Prussia to the main body of the Reich. If she were allowed to have Danzig, the Poles claimed, she would soon also have this strip, and Poland would be a land-locked country like Hungary. For this reason the Poles prepared to fight the minute Germany attempted to occupy the Free City. To them the defense of their Corridor to the sea was the defense of their independence.

Realizing this, France and Great Britain both promised to come to Poland's aid if Germany took any steps which Poland believed threatened her independence. Early on the morning of September 1, 1939, Germany took such a step. The result, as everyone knows, was a new European war.

IN HUNGARY

The half million Germans in Hungary (map, p. 43) have been thoroughly penetrated by National Socialism. But the Nazi drive did not stop there. The Swabians (Germans) were only the advance guard of Nazism along the middle Danube. The Nazis made startling inroads among certain elements of the Magyars too. Their most sensational progress was made in the ranks of the landless Hungarian peasants. Landless Swabians and Magyars alike listened to the propaganda of Hitler's agents, who promised that when the Nazis ruled Hungary the large estates would be broken up and the land divided among the poor. To the landless peasants this lure was very effective.

Before the German annexation, Austria acted as a buffer between Hungary and the Reich. So the Hungarians could show a certain amount of independence toward Germany. Since the fall of Austria, however, Hungary has had a common frontier with the Reich, and there are German troops along the Hungarian border. Consequently, inasmuch as Hungary is a small country, she hardly dares to take a stand that might bring reprisals from her powerful neighbor.

IN RUMANIA

We have already mentioned the large German minority in Rumania. Most of these Germans live in Transylvania and the Banat (map, p. 45), on the route from the Reich to the Rumanian oil fields which Hitler covets. As we have seen, these Germans have been organized and drilled in their role as shock troops of Pan-Germanism. During 1938, however, King Carol suddenly adopted a vigorous policy toward the Iron Guard, the pro-Nazi and Fascist groups and the Nazi members of the German minority. The King and his supporters had come to realize that there was danger from these reactionary forces within the kingdom. Of course, today there is also danger from without.

The German, Magyar and Bulgarian minorities in Rumania all have marked leanings toward Germany, Hungary and Bulgaria respectively. Furthermore, we know that in the months before the present war began Hitler was using Hungary and Bulgaria as threats to Rumania. In other words, through them he was exerting pressure upon King Carol. So we may be sure that he was missing no opportunity to use these three minorities in his drive to make Rumania into a German colony.

IN YUGOSLAVIA

The German minority in Yugoslavia was not so troublesome as the German minorities in several other countries. This was due largely to the watchful attitude of the Yugoslav government and police. When the Germans showed signs of political activity, the police often took stern measures.

But, mainly for reasons of power politics, Hitler directed his policies among the German minority in Yugoslavia along non-violent lines. For several years he commanded his followers in the South Slav kingdom to cooperate with the government. More could be accomplished there, he believed, by working from inside the government than from the opposition. So for the time being the German minority in Yugoslavia made no serious trouble. But that policy could change suddenly.

IN FRANCE

We don't hear much about the German minority in the French provinces of Alsace and Lorraine (map, p. 27), but that is largely because France treats her German minority well. As a result the Germans in France have little cause for complaint. Besides, many Alsatians are really neither German nor French, but a mixed people. Moreover, the Germans in France believed that in case of war between the Reich and France, the early battles, at least, might be fought in the territory where they lived. Another important reason was that Hitler was concentrating his attention on Eastern Europe and wanted no war with France until he had consolidated his position there.

Yet, even so, there was some political activity among the German minority in France's eastern provinces. This activity took the form mainly of underground agitation for autonomy. This agitation met no favorable response among the French people. They knew that to grant autonomy to Alsace and Lorraine would mean to open the gates to Nazi propaganda, perhaps even to another German invasion. Moreover, it would have imperiled the famed Maginot line of French fortifications, which would then be located in autonomous territory. Consequently France turned a stern face toward the east and discouraged propaganda in favor of autonomy within the Republic.

IN BELGIUM

Before we complete our tour of the German minorities, we must mention the Germans in Belgium. The peace treaties gave some former German territory to the Belgians. The Reich lost thereby about 75,000 people. Not all of them, of course, were

Germans. Most of the German minority in Belgium lives in the vicinity of Eupen, Malmédy and Moresnet. These Germans are located in border areas where the population is mixed (center map). Although it is small, the German minority in Belgium provides the Nazis with an excuse to intervene in Belgian affairs whenever it suits Hitler's purpose to do so.

IN THE UKRAINE

In recent years we have heard much about the Ukraine and the Ukrainian minorities. As we have already seen, the Ukrainians are divided among four countries: the Soviet Union, Poland, Rumania and Hungary (map. p. 91).

Before the World War nearly all the Ukrainians lived in the two great empires of Russia and Austria-Hungary. Since the war many Ukrainians have been demanding the right of "self-determination." There has been frequent trouble between the Ukrainian minority and the Polish authorities. There have been separatist movements in the Soviet Ukraine that have brought severe reprisals against the Ukrainian nationalists. The Ukrainians (Ruthenians) of Czechoslovakia seem to have been the best satisfied group of that scattered people. But after the Munich "peace with honor" even the Ruthenians began thinking in terms of a greater Ukraine. Their absorption by Hungary, however, has been followed by severe repression of their nationalist movement.

THE NAZIS AND THE UKRAINE

As long as comparatively normal conditions prevailed in Europe, there seemed to be small chance that the Ukrainian nationalists could establish an independent state. But when Hitler came to power in the Reich, the situation changed. Those of us who have read *Mein Kampf* know that the Nazis have long planned to create a great empire in the East. That means, among other things, the acquisition of lands inhabited by Ukrainians.

Now in each of the Ukrainian areas in Russia, Poland, Rumania and Hungary there is a German minority—that is, a minority within a minority (map, p. 27). But we are not so much interested in these small Germanic islands. As they were not large enough to give Hitler much help, he went after the Ukrainians themselves. German radio stations sent out propaganda programs in the Ukrainian language. These programs were intended especially for the Ukrainians in Poland; but some of them may have reached the Soviet Union. Before the present war began there was a Ukrainian bureau in Berlin. An organization of Ukrainian officers existed on German soil. They were being trained for the day when they could take the field against Poland and perhaps the Soviet Union.

WHY THE NAZIS WANTED AN INDEPENDENT UKRAINE

Germany wanted a so-called "independent" Ukrainian state under her influence. Such a state could provide the Reich with much of the food and raw materials that Germany needs so badly. And it could provide a large market for German manufactured goods. Moreover, the creation of such a state would weaken Poland and the Soviet Union, thereby tipping the European balance of power still further in favor of the Reich.

The Ukrainian leaders may have been entirely sincere and patriotic nationalists. But their activities played directly into the hands of the Nazi imperialists. The Poles and Russians, however, had no intention of permitting the Ukrainians to form a new state. They fought the Nazi-directed Ukrainian secessionist drive.

HITLER'S HUMAN DYNAMITE

These, then, are the principal minorities which constituted Hitler's human dynamite in Europe. Hitler was like a man sitting

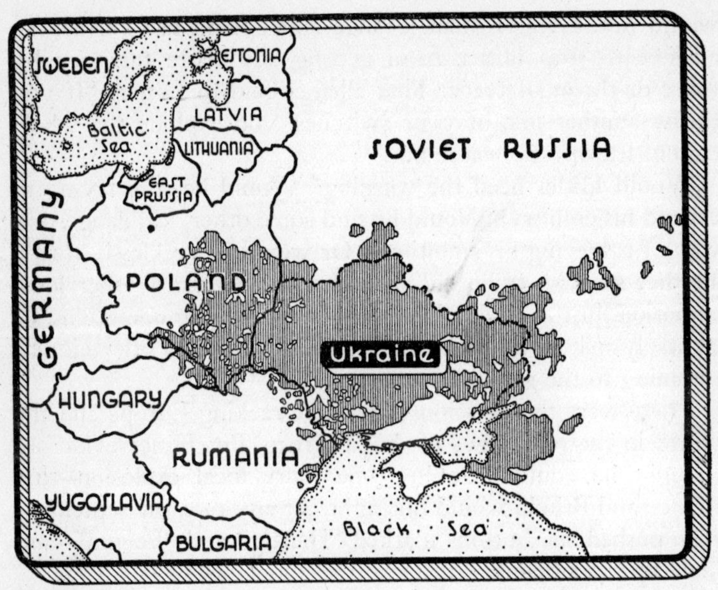

THE UKRAINIAN MINORITIES

at an electric panel. On the panel were many switches. Each switch was connected with a powerful charge of dynamite somewhere on the map of Europe—some minority group or other which was like a great mine that could be set off at a touch of the right switch. When he thought the time was ripe Hitler reached out and threw one of those switches. Instantly there was a deafening explosion somewhere outside the borders of the Reich. And when the broken rock had fallen and the dirt and dust had cleared away the map of Europe was seen to have changed again.

At least that was the way it had worked in the past. That was the way it worked in Austria. That was the way it worked in Czechoslovakia. And that is the way it worked in Memelland. Would it work again without a war? Many people thought it would not. Great Britain, France and Poland had formed an alliance to stop Hitler from getting any more territory by force or threat of force. That alliance said to Hitler: "If you throw another one of your switches, you explode the whole map of Europe. So watch out."

Would Hitler heed the warning? Would he stop trying to expand his country? Would he find some other, less dangerous, way of achieving his ambitions? Or would he recklessly throw another switch? If he did, would there be just another local explosion, just another of his well-timed blasting operations, or a cataclysmic earthquake that might bring even Hitler himself tumbling to the ground?

These were the questions that were racking Europe and the world in the tense days of August 1939. But Hitler evidently thought he could have just one more local explosion—that France and Britain would not fight. At any rate, on September 1 he pushed the buttons marked "Danzig" and "Poland"—and blew up a continent.

XI. The Solution

The purpose of this book has been to give you an outline history of the minority problem and to describe the extremely complicated minority situation that exists in Europe today.

In the course of our study we have learned that there is no panacea for the minority problem: there is no easy way out. For each minority situation in Europe is a little bit different from the one a few miles away. There are contradictions on every hand. There are conflicting statistics and there are claims and counter-claims. Consequently it is not always possible to find out the truth, and one cannot be arbitrary in apportioning praise and blame. In many cases, no doubt, both sides sincerely believe in their contentions. So we cannot be dogmatic when we are discussing such an inextricable tangle of age-old conflicts as these. For no human being can know even a majority of the answers to these problems which spring up everywhere to create economic disorder and the threat of war.

FOUR TRUTHS ABOUT THE MINORITY PROBLEM

But we can set down some conclusions that will hardly be disputed.

In the first place, we have learned that in one part of Europe after another it is impossible to draw a satisfactory frontier through mixed nationality areas. For the existence of minority "islands" makes it impossible.

Second, we have seen examples of the exchange of minorities, and we know that it would be impracticable to attempt to repeat these migrations on a scale large enough to relieve Europe's minority problems. So nearly all the minority peoples must stay where they are, in the lands they and their forebears have inhabited for centuries.

The third point follows from these. It is that there is no way by which everybody can attain "self-determination." For self-determination for one people may mean the invasion of another people's rights, and if we tried to give every people in Europe the free rein of geographical self-determination the result would be something very much like anarchy.

But, fourth, the persecution or repression of minorities is no solution either. Perhaps the best that can be said of it is that sooner or later it is almost certain to react against the majority applying it.

THE SOLUTION

What, then, is the solution?

Well, as we have seen, there are several types of minorities. There are the religious minorities, those whose only difference from the majority is a religious difference. Then there are the minorities of opinion, those which differ from the majority peoples in their political, social or economic opinions. Finally, there are the minorities which differ from the majorities in ancestry, language and culture—the so-called "national" or cultural minorities.

The problem of the religious minorities may be solved by generous provisions for religious equality and the abolition of all discrimination against persons differing in their religion from the majority, or dominant, peoples.

The problem of the minorities of opinion may be solved by democracy, which permits every one to express his views on political, social or economic questions without hindrance.

The problem of national or cultural minorities may be solved, not by territorial adjustments, which only turn the tables and create new minorities, but by autonomy and federation within the existing states. In other words, these minority groups may be granted the freedom to speak their own languages, adhere to their own national traditions and cultures, even, to a large extent, to manage their own local affairs, without changing any boundaries at all.

A good example of this solution in operation is Switzerland. If it works there, it can, with the will to make it work, be made to work elsewhere. And if it were once successfully applied to Europe's minority problems, it would not only create better feeling between the minority and the majority peoples but would also improve the relations between the various European governments.

With half Europe at war, these suggestions may seem utopian, to say the least. But when the war is over, and the new peace conference meets, it will be confronted, as the Paris Peace Conference was, with this age-old problem of minorities. Unless it finds a thoroughgoing solution such as that suggested above, it will fail, as the Paris Peace Conference failed, and, sooner or later, Europe will once again be at war.

SUGGESTED READING

BUELL, R. L. *Poland: Key to Europe.* Chapters ix-xi. New York. Knopf. 1939.

"Calling America." *Survey Graphic.* February 1939. (Special issue on minorities and refugees, with many illustrations.)

DEAN, V. M. "Europe's Explosive Minorities." *New Republic.* April 12, 1939.

JANOWSKY, O. I. *The Jews and Minority Rights.* New York. Columbia University Press. 1933.

JANOWSKY, O. I. *People at Bay.* New York. Oxford University Press. 1938.

JUNGHANN, OTTO. *National Minorities in Europe.* New York. Covici, Friede. 1932.

LENGYEL, EMIL. *The Cauldron Boils.* New York. Dial Press. 1932.

MACARTNEY, C. A. *National States and National Minorities.* Royal Institute of International Affairs. London. Oxford University Press. 1934.

SETON-WATSON, R. W. *Britain and the Dictators.* New York. Macmillan. 1938.

SIMONDS, F. H. *Can Europe Keep the Peace?* Revised edition. New York. Harper. 1934.

STONE, SHEPARD. *Shadow Over Europe.* Headline Book No. 15. Revised edition. New York. Foreign Policy Association. 1939.

WOLFE, H. C. *The German Octopus.* New York. Doubleday Doran. 1938.

A NOTE ON HEADLINE BOOKS

Human Dynamite is one of the Foreign Policy Association's HEADLINE BOOKS. The object of the series is to provide sufficient unbiased background information to enable readers to reach intelligent and independent conclusions on the important international problems of the day. HEADLINE BOOKS are prepared under the supervision of the Department of Popular Education of the Foreign Policy Association with the cooperation of the Association's Research Staff of experts.

The Foreign Policy Association is a non-profit American organization founded "to carry on research and educational activities to aid in the understanding and constructive development of American foreign policy." It is an impartial research organization and does not seek to promote any one point of view toward international affairs. Such views as may be expressed or implied in any of its publications are those of the author and not of the Association.

For further information about HEADLINE BOOKS and the other publications of the Foreign Policy Association, write to the Department of Popular Education, Foreign Policy Association, 8 West 40th Street, New York, N. Y.

ABOUT THE AUTHOR

Henry C. Wolfe is a well-known writer and lecturer on European affairs. He has traveled extensively in Central and Eastern Europe and has published many newspaper and magazine articles on conditions there. His first book, on Nazi foreign policy, was published in 1938 under the title of *The German Octopus*.

Both author and publisher wish to thank Professor Oscar I. Janowsky, of the College of the City of New York, for his invaluable assistance in the preparation of the manuscript.